YOU CHOOSE BOOKS™

CAN YOU

SURVIVE?

CAPSTONE PRESS
a capstone imprint

You Choose Books are published by Capstone Press,
1710 Roe Crest Drive, North Mankato, Minnesota 56003.
www.mycapstone.com

Library of Congress Cataloging-in-Publication Data
Cataloging-in-publication information is on file with the Library of Congress.
ISBN 978-1-51579-081-5 (paperback)

Photo Credits

Alamy: Arcticphoto/Bryan and Cherry Alexander, 168, Classic Image, 122, imagebroker, 308, Mary Evans Picture Library, 128, mediacolor's, 322, OLIVIER CELERIER, 234, Photos 12, 140; Capstone: 120, 226, 301, Rod Whigham, 21; Capstone Studio: Karon Dubke, Cover Bottom Right, Cover Back Right; Courtesy of the National Science Foundation, U.S. Antarctic Program: Photograph by Emily Stone, 215, Kristan Hutchison, 184, Peter Rejcek, 187, 210, 213, Robert Schwarz, 171, Stacy Kim, 182; Dreamstime: Willtu, 73; Getty Images: Bettmann, 124, Central Press, 137, Danny Lehman, 230, Gallo Images/Fiona McIntosh, 154, General Photographic Agency, 152, National Geographic/ James P. Blair, 258, Per-Anders Pettersson, 290, Sygma/John Van Hassel, 175, Sygma/ Stephane Cardinale, 157, 181; Newscom: Photoshot/Xinhua/Zhang Honkxiang, 304, ZUMA Press/I75, 299; Photo Researchers, Inc: Dan Suzio, 265; Seth White: 195; Shutterstock/Alin Popescu, 107, AMA, 99, Anelina, 57, Arne Bramsen, 28, Christa DeRidder, 248, Darren Baker, Cover Bottom Left, Cover Back Left, David Wingate, 38, Dennis W Donohue, 243, doodle, 104, edella, 80, Eric Gevaert, 76, evantravels, 272, Forbis, Back Cover Top, 86, Galyna Andrushko, Cover Top, 228, 288, Gary Yim, 254, Jason Swarr, 262, Kanwarjit Singh Boparai, 279, Karen Kean, 116, kkaplin, 118, Luisa Amare, 79, Mark Skalny, 256, Marty Wakat, 63, Pascal RATEAU, 292, pashabo, Design Element, Pichugin Dmitry, 313, PT Images, 92, RCPPHOTO, 43, Rich Carey, 8, rSnapshotPhotos, 14, Sebastian Duda, 10, Sebastien Burel, 320, Steve Bower, 283, Steve Byland, 275, Ventura, 46, vilainecrevette, 13, Vladimir Melnik, 252, Vladimir Wrangel, 318, Wilson Chan, 224, Yarik, 287, Yellowj, Cover Bottom Right Background, Cover Back Right Background; Super Stock Inc.: age fotostock, Cover Bottom Middle, Cover Back Middle; U.S. Army Survival Manual FM 21-76: 35

Printed in China.
030217   004427

TABLE OF CONTENTS

Can You Survive
BEING
Lost AT Sea?

An Interactive Survival Adventure

by Allison Lassieur

Consultant:
Howard Reichert, Member
Storm Trysail Foundation
Larchmont, New York

TABLE OF CONTENTS

About Your
ADVENTURE

YOU are sailing on the ocean when something suddenly goes wrong. You're at the mercy of storms, dehydration, and sharks. How will you stay alive?

In this book you'll deal with extreme survival situations. You'll explore how the knowledge you have and the choices you make can mean the difference between life and death.

Chapter One sets the scene. Then you choose which path to read. Follow the directions at the bottom of each page. The choices you make will change your outcome. After you finish one path, go back and read the others for new perspectives and more adventures.

YOU CHOOSE the path
you take through your adventure.

Sharp coral reefs
can sometimes cause
boat accidents.

CHAPTER 1

Danger at Sea

It happens in a blink—a freak wave, an unexpected accident, a fast-moving storm. Suddenly a pleasant day on the ocean turns into a nightmare of survival.

Of all the places in the world to be lost, the sea is the worst. At sea, there is no food, water, or shelter of any kind, other than what you manage to have with you. You're exposed to extreme heat and cold, as well as storms, waves, and wind. Most people who die at sea don't drown. They die of starvation, dehydration, or hypothermia.

It seems odd that you could die of thirst in a huge ocean of water. Ocean water is about three times saltier than your blood. That makes it impossible for your body to process safely.

Turn the page.

In case of emergency, the sail of a sailboat can be used for shelter from wind and rain.

A few swallows of saltwater will make you feel sick and vomit. More than that will causes seizures, brain damage, hallucinations, and death. Finding fresh water is necessary for survival.

The second most important thing, after finding fresh water, is protection from the elements. The heat from the sun and the ocean winds will dehydrate you and make your skin burn, blister, and crack. Extra clothing, plastic tarps, rubber mats, life jackets, rugs, or even seaweed can help shield you.

A big problem for anyone lost at sea is hypothermia, which occurs when your core body temperature drops below 95 degrees Fahrenheit. You lose the most heat through your head, arms, legs, and groin. The best way to avoid hypothermia is to get out of the water.

Turn the page.

Water and shelter will keep you alive for a few days, but after that you'll have to find food. Anything edible will keep you alive, including fish, birds, and seaweed. But not all sea creatures are safe to eat. Puffer fish and jellyfish can be deadly. It's important to know which fish will keep you alive and which fish will poison you.

Even if the odds are in your favor, it's your will to live that will end up deciding your fate. If you have that, along with clear thinking and skill, it's likely you'll survive being lost at sea.

A jellyfish's sting is painful and can be deadly.

To be downed in a small aircraft at sea, turn to page **15**.

To be adrift in a sailboat with a small crew in the Caribbean, turn to page **47**.

To be lost at sea alone along the Atlantic coast, turn to page **81**.

Small airplanes usually have only one engine.

CHAPTER 2

Crash Landing

You walk across the small airport tarmac and take a look back at the evening sunset. You've spent the summer hiking, swimming, and relaxing with your family on this remote Canadian island. It's time for you to get back to school on the mainland, so you're leaving a few days early.

The small 10-seater airplane quickly fills up with other vacationers on their way home. You stash your backpack under the seat, strap on your seatbelt, and settle in. There's a sign overhead that says everyone must put on a life jacket. No one else has one on, so you don't bother. You doze off, barely feeling the plane taxi down the runway and lift into the sky.

Turn the page.

A shaking sensation wakes you. You're horrified to realize that it's the plane that's shaking. Your heart hammers in your chest, but you try to stay calm. Miles of ocean stretch below with no land in sight. The engine makes a loud coughing sound as the plane continues to drop. The water is getting closer. You hear the pilot, Sam, over the intercom.

"We're going to hit, folks. Brace yourselves."

You put your head between your knees, grasping your legs with your arms. Everyone else does the same. The plane's engine whines loudly, and then you hear a loud explosion. Something hits the back of your head, knocking you unconscious.

You wake up minutes later. The plane is in the ocean, broken into sections. The part you're in is sinking fast. Your head is throbbing from the injury. Sputtering as you swallow the cold water, you flip the seat belt buckle and swim free.

Then you remember your backpack. There's a bottle of water, some trail mix, your wallet, and a wad of dirty clothes inside.

To look for your backpack, turn to page 18.

To leave it behind and swim away from the wreckage, turn to page 21.

You don't have to search long. The backpack is floating a few feet away. You wrap one strap around your wrist and swim away from the plane's wreckage.

The choppy waves make you feel sick to your stomach. A large chunk of the plane floats past, and you manage to grab it. This is good—staying afloat is key to survival. Too bad you didn't grab your life jacket when you had the chance.

A familiar smell stings your nose and burns your throat. Fuel! It must be leaking out of the airplane. If it catches fire, you're in trouble. But you want to stay close to the plane to salvage anything useful and find any other survivors.

To swim clear of the fuel, go to page **19**.

To stay with the plane, turn to page **34**.

Taking a deep breath, you dip your head beneath the water and swim away from the fuel slick. When you come up for air, you're clear. By now it's almost dark.

"Help me!" someone shouts from somewhere in front of you.

Sure enough, you see a dark figure waving his arms. He goes under the waves and then comes up, sputtering.

"Help!" he cries again, but it's much fainter. He's drowning. Drowning people are dangerous. In their panic, they could drown anyone trying to rescue them. You have to be careful about how you approach him.

To swim around behind him, turn to page 20.

To swim directly to the drowning man, turn to page 35.

You swim around and surface behind the man. As he goes under, you pull him up by the hair, ducking his flailing arms. Grabbing him under the armpits, you swim backward, pulling his face out of the water. He's coughing and vomiting, but he's alive. After a few strokes you stop, exhausted. The man has relaxed. He says his name is Bill.

"Thanks," Bill gasps between gulps of air. "I can't believe I panicked like that."

Just then you both see a flashing light. Shouts ring out over the water.

"Is anyone out there?"

Together you start yelling as loudly as you can. A large rubber life raft looms out of the darkness. A life preserver lands near you both with a splash.

Turn to page 25.

You don't want to be near the plane when it sinks. You could get tangled in debris and pulled under. Slowly you swim out into the sea. You bump into something in the water. It's your backpack! A seat cushion is tangled in its straps.

You slide the backpack over your arm and grab the cushion to your chest. Then you pull your legs up. This position is called the Heat Escaping Lessening Posture, or HELP for short. But you can't hold that position for long. You stretch out in the water with the cushion tucked under your chin.

The HELP position helps conserve body heat in cold water.

Turn the page.

You have no idea how long you've been in the water, but it's probably no more than an hour. You're lightheaded from your head injury. All the seawater you've swallowed comes up in a wave of nausea. It's hard to think clearly. Becoming disoriented and having hallucinations are symptoms of hypothermia, but you don't feel that cold. Besides, it's still summer.

You feel sleepy, but you shake yourself awake. You need to move to warm your muscles. From somewhere you remember that moving is bad because it uses more body heat than being still. But to your confused mind, that doesn't seem right.

To remain still, go to page 23.

To get moving to stay warm, turn to page 36.

Slowly, painfully, you pull your knees back into your chest and float upright. You fight to stay conscious, but your thoughts are jumbled and don't make any sense. You remember a grizzly bear you saw on vacation. Suddenly there it is, in the water in front of you!

"Are you OK?" the bear says. Then the bear starts shaking you—hard. You take a swing at it, and then the fog lifts from your mind. The bear turns into a man hanging onto a large piece of debris.

"I guess not," you reply shakily. "I thought you were a bear."

The man chokes out a laugh. "Hypothermia. We need to get you out of the water."

Turn the page.

The man tells you his name is Bill. He swims behind you and helps you scramble onto a piece of debris. The air feels freezing, but you know it's warmer than the water. You lie there, teeth chattering, until you notice a flashing light not too far away. At first you think it's another hallucination. Then it flashes again. In the brief flash of light, you see a large rubber raft inching toward you. "Help! Help!" you and Bill cry.

Strong hands lift you out of the water. You're wrapped in something dry and warm. Someone presses a plastic water bottle to your lips. You drink thirstily. Then someone opens your mouth and presses a pill under your tongue.

"For seasickness," a voice you recognize says. "Let it dissolve."

It's Sam, the pilot!

"I'm glad to see you," you say.

"Good to see you too," Sam replies, examining your head wound. "I don't think this is too bad," he says, popping open a first-aid kit. He wipes away the caked blood with an antiseptic pad.

Now that you're out of the water and hydrated, you're feeling much better. Bill and two other survivors huddle in blankets in the raft. With you and Sam, that makes five survivors. Six are still missing.

Turn the page.

"We found five who didn't make it," Sam says sadly. "There's only one more." After you strap on a life jacket, Sam hands you a flashlight. Together you sweep the ocean and debris looking for the other passenger.

Your flashlight moves over a bit of bright red fabric. A jacket—and someone's in it. "There!" you say. The figure lifts her head weakly.

"She's floating!" you yell. The woman is doing the dead man's float to conserve her energy.

Sam throws the life preserver, which is attached to a rope, into the water. The woman tries to grab the preserver, but she can't move her arms well. She tries again and misses. A wave pushes her farther out.

"I'll go get her," you say, jumping into the water before Sam can protest.

To grab the life preserver first, go to page **27**.

To swim out to the woman, turn to page **37**.

As you swim toward the woman, you grab the rope that's attached to the life preserver and follow it out. When you get to the woman, she's not moving.

"Grab the life preserver!" you say, pushing it to her. She lifts one arm, and then lets it fall weakly back into the water.

"You can do this," you shout. "Don't die here!" Being careful to not get too close, you put her hands on the life preserver. She revives and clutches it to her chest in a tight grip.

"That's it," you say. "Hang on, and we'll be in the raft in no time."

Sam pulls you both in, and you immediately wrap her in a blanket and give her water.

"Thanks," the woman says. "I'm Emma." You'd like to tell her everything's going to be OK, but you're not sure that's true.

Turn the page.

A tarp and a rope are important tools for sea survival.

When Emma is comfortable, you approach Sam. "Is help coming?" you ask quietly.

"I hope so," he says. "We were off course when the plane crashed, so it might be a few hours. When it's light, we need to take an inventory of supplies and build an anchor so we don't drift."

Curling up under a blanket, you try to get some sleep. The rising sun wakes you. You're terribly thirsty and still nauseous, but alive. So far.

To inventory the supplies, go to page 29.

To build the anchor, turn to page 38.

You take note of everything in the raft. There's a small pile of salvaged stuff, including a few seat cushions, clothing, a small cooler, a couple of plastic jugs, and a broken mirror. The cooler contains several soggy sandwiches, a few cans of soda, some water, and a jar of olives. You give Sam a jug to fill with ocean water for an anchor. You also show him what's in your backpack.

"The extra clothing will be good protection," he says. The raft kit contains a plastic tarp, emergency rations, three gallons of fresh water, the thermal blankets that Sam gave out, and a two-way radio. You get excited when you find the radio, but Sam shakes his head.

"Not working," he says. "The crash must have broken it. I'm sure we'll be rescued within the next 24 hours, but we should figure out the rations for a week." Even with the water and trail mix from your backpack, there isn't enough for six people.

Turn the page.

"Don't worry, it'll keep us alive," Sam says. "A person can survive on four ounces of water a day. It won't be fun, though."

By now the sun is high in the sky. The other passengers are stirring. Together you and Sam divide the rations so that everyone will have food and water for seven days. Then you pass out the day's rations to everyone.

"Don't drink your water ration today if you can help it," Sam says. "Right now, we have plenty of water in our systems. We'll need this water later in case …" He doesn't finish the sentence.

The day gets hot, so you all rig the plastic tarp over your heads to shield you from the sun. The sea is rough, and the raft plunges and dips in the waves. It's exhausting to hang on to keep from being flung overboard. The saltwater spray dries out your skin despite the tarps, and the heat is relentless.

You expect rescue any moment, but evening comes and you're still drifting. You've never felt so hungry and thirsty in your life. From the expressions on everyone else's faces, they feel the same way.

"Come on, Sam," says Bill. "The rescuers have to be on their way. Let us have the rest of the food and water."

"Yes, I'm sure we'll be rescued soon," says another man, Mike.

Sam is clearly uncomfortable. "It's not a good idea," he says.

"Let's have them," Mike says in a menacing tone.

Sam looks hard at the two men, and then silently passes out everyone's rations. They gobble and gulp hungrily, but you hesitate.

To eat your rations at once, turn to page 32.

To save your food and water, turn to page 41.

There's no way rescue isn't coming soon, you think as you eat all your food and drink most of the water. You feel full and comfortable for the first time since the crash. Everyone is in good spirits, and there's a lot of laughter and talk as evening comes.

The next day dawns bright. Everyone is still excited at the idea of rescue. As the day stretches on, though, conversation dies down. People try to nap under the tarp, and a few jump into the water to cool off. You know that's a bad idea because you need to conserve all your energy. Instead you dampen your clothing with a little seawater and put as many clothes on as you can stand. This cools you down and helps avoid heatstroke.

Staying still will conserve energy, and what better way to do that than to relax and sleep? You crawl under the tarp and try to nap. As the sun slips down on the horizon, your heart sinks. Another night at sea—and now with no food or water.

By morning everyone is half-crazed with thirst. You look at the sky, hoping to see rain clouds. If it rains, the tarp will catch the fresh water. But there's not a cloud in the blue sky.

Emma is the first one to drink ocean water. Mike, Bill, and the other survivor, Sarah, drink it too. Watching them gulp water makes you even thirstier. Seawater can make you sick at best, and kill you at worst. But if the rescuers are on their way, surely they'll be here long before the seawater can kill you.

To drink seawater, turn to page **40**.

To wait longer before drinking, turn to page **44**.

It's important to keep the fuel out of your eyes. You hold your head high above the water and kick toward a pile of debris near the plane's wing. It's almost dark, but you can see a seat cushion floating nearby. You grab it. Underneath the wing you see what looks like a blue cooler bobbing in the water. It could have food, water, or medical supplies inside.

Sparks pop and fly out from the wreckage. At first you think the loud WOOSH you hear is the ocean wind hitting your face. But the wind is hot, and the surface of the water around you bursts into flames. What's left of the plane explodes as a fireball of red flames and black smoke surrounds you. Lucky for you, the pain only lasts a few seconds before you sink beneath the ocean's surface for the last time.

34

THE END

To follow another path, turn to page 13
To read the conclusion, turn to page 105.

"I'm coming!" you shout as you swim to the drowning man. Just as he goes under again, he grabs your shoulders and pushes you under in his panic. You let go of the backpack, trying to get away. He's strong, and he tries to climb on top of you, pushing you down farther. You're too exhausted to fight his strength, so you stop struggling. Both of you quickly sink to the bottom of the sea.

Rescue a drowning victim by throwing a floatable object to them.

THE END

To follow another path, turn to page 13.
To read the conclusion, turn to page 105.

It's hard to concentrate. In your confused state, you decide that it's foolish to stay in one place. Quickly you toss the backpack away and kick off your shoes, pants, and jacket. The water seems even warmer now that you're free of all those clothes.

From across the dark water you hear laughter and see lights. It must be a party on the plane, and they've started without you. "I'm coming!" you shout and start swimming. But the sounds keep moving around, and it's confusing. You swim one way, then another, but the water is choppy and you don't seem to get any closer to the party.

It's a lot easier to swim underwater, you realize happily. If you dive under, the waves will carry you right to the party. Without another thought, that's exactly what you do. You don't realize that you'll never make it back to the surface again.

THE END

To follow another path, turn to page 13.
To read the conclusion, turn to page 105.

The woman is alive but not moving. You unclip your life jacket and try to put it on her, but she's heavy and the waves are too strong. Finally you tie it around her chest.

As you turn to drag her back to the life raft, she revives and begins to scream. Panicked, she grabs you around the neck, pounding your wounded head. The force of the blows knock you out, and you sink under the dark waves.

THE END

To follow another path, turn to page 13.
To read the conclusion, turn to page 105.

Most life rafts inflate automatically and do not have a motor.

You need to figure out something that will create drag on the raft and prevent it from drifting too far away from the crash site. Sam gives you a length of rope, but what is there to use for the anchor? Looking around, you spot the cooler. After you tie the rope to the cooler, you and Sam throw it overboard. As it hits the water, the cooler comes untied.

Quickly you put on a life jacket. When you reach the cooler, you tie your knots correctly this time. As you start to swim back to the raft, you feel something tug lightly at your ankle. When you try to shake it off, it tightens around your leg.

You take a deep breath and dive underwater. Floating a few feet below you is a huge tangle of fish net, buoys, dead fish, and other debris. Somehow you managed to put your foot through a piece of the net. As you work on the jumble around your leg, the strong current catches the net and pulls it, taking you with it. You're dragged down so fast that you don't have time to be scared.

THE END

To follow another path, turn to page 13.
To read the conclusion, turn to page 105.

The salty ocean water tastes terrible, but it's cool and wet. You take tiny sips, hoping that it will keep you alive and not make you too sick.

It's not long before everyone starts vomiting. The raft fills with the smells and sounds of sickness. As the day goes on, some people drink more seawater. Some even drink their own urine, but they quickly vomit it up.

You vomit over the side of the raft and close your eyes. You never imagined your great summer island vacation would end like this. As you slip into unconsciousness, you hope rescuers will find your body so your family can give you a decent funeral.

THE END

To follow another path, turn to page 13.
To read the conclusion, turn to page 105.

It takes all your willpower to eat only one ration and stash the rest in your backpack. When no one is looking, you hide your backpack behind the seat cushions. Sam sees you and nods in agreement.

By the next afternoon everyone is desperately thirsty. Emma, the woman you rescued, wants to drink seawater. You and the others talk her out of it. "Let's try use the tarp to catch condensed dew overnight," Sam suggests.

You tie the tarp corners to the raft and weigh down the center with a plastic jug of seawater. Then you position the cooler underneath the tarp, below the jug. Your hope is that dew will run down the sides of the tarp and drip into the cooler.

There isn't any water in the cooler the next morning. Now no one can stop Emma. She takes huge gulps of seawater. Over the next few hours, the other passengers join her.

Turn the page.

You want to drink the saltwater so badly that you sit on your hands and bite your cracked lips to stop yourself. Sam puts a hand on your shoulder and smiles encouragingly.

It doesn't take long for everyone to start vomiting. They're not paying any attention to you, so you quietly eat a mouthful of food. Sam does the same. You curl into a ball and try to sleep, ignoring the moaning and vomiting.

When you wake up in the morning, the raft is bobbing lightly on the water. Then you realize that the raft is empty except for you and Sam. Frantically you rush to the side of the raft and scan the ocean for signs of anyone.

"They're all gone," Sam says through cracked lips. "The hallucinations from the cold and drinking saltwater got to them. Bill jumped first, then everyone else tried to save him."

You bow your head, filled with despair. You know that you and Sam can't survive much longer out here. Just then, you see something in the sky. Could it be? Yes, it's a helicopter!

"Look!" you shout, grabbing the piece of broken mirror. You angle it so that it flashes in the sunlight. Sam grabs the tarp and waves it with all the strength he has left. The helicopter turns and heads toward you! You can't believe your terrible ordeal is over.

The U.S. Coast Guard uses the HH-60J Jayhawk helicopter for search and rescue.

THE END

To follow another path, turn to page 13.
To read the conclusion, turn to page 105.

All around you, the other survivors are vomiting up seawater. Some people even drink their own urine, but that quickly comes back up as well. The inside of your dry mouth feels sticky. Your skin turns dry and shriveled, and you stop sweating. A dizzying headache throbs between your eyes. So this is what dehydration and starvation feel like.

Your thoughts are jumbled and confused, but somehow you hang onto the thought that "seawater is bad to drink." All your thoughts focus on that one idea, and you start mumbling it out loud. Somehow just saying it over and over makes things better.

Time seems to stop. You curl up in the bottom of the raft and repeat, "seawater is bad to drink" over and over. You don't even notice when Sam squeezes a few drops of fresh water into your cracked lips. Or the next day when several pairs of hands lift you in the air and load you into a rescue helicopter.

You wake up the next day in a hospital bed. The decision not to drink the saltwater helped you and Sam survive your ordeal. Sadly, the rest of the castaways weren't so lucky.

THE END

To follow another path, turn to page 13.
To read the conclusion, turn to page 105.

Sailboats use the force of lift to move through the water.

CHAPTER 3

Adrift in Paradise

You can't believe you're here. Learning to scuba dive has always been your dream. You spent last winter taking lessons. Now you're on a chartered sailboat in the Caribbean with four other divers and the captain, Andy. It's the vacation of a lifetime.

When the boat left harbor three days ago, the ocean was clear and smooth. But now big clouds are gathering on the horizon. The water is choppy, but not too rough. Andy says he's gotten several reports saying the weather is fine. He's an experienced sailor. You're sure he knows what he's doing.

Everyone gathers to enjoy a delicious seafood meal. After dinner, you ask Andy about tomorrow's dive.

Turn the page.

"There's a beautiful section of coral reef I want to show you," he says. "But it's a few hours' sail away. We'll get there by morning if we do a night sail." He shows you a printout. "This is the latest news about the weather. There's a small storm in that area, but it should move through before we get there."

After more conversation, Andy says good night and goes to the wheelhouse. The other passengers say their good nights and go to their berths below the deck. You're not tired, but if you're going to spend all day tomorrow diving, you should probably join them.

To go to your bunk, go to page **49**.

To stay on deck, turn to page **54**.

It seems as if you've just fallen asleep when someone is shaking you.

"Get up!" It's Kat, one of the other divers. "We've got to get out of here!"

You jump out of your berth into several inches of water on the floor. The boat is rocking so hard that you lose your balance and fall. It must be really bad out there. You pull on a shirt and jeans. Over that, you put on your all-weather jacket. You could grab a few more things, but it might be better to head to the deck as fast as possible. Kat's disappeared. She's probably trying to wake the others.

To go straight to the deck, turn to page 50.

To collect a few belongings, turn to page 68.

Seconds may mean the difference between life and death. You head straight for the deck. You're halfway up the ladder when a huge wave hits the boat, sending it rolling. Fortunately your grip is strong, and you don't fall. You hear a yell behind you. It's Ben, one of the divers. The rushing water is pushing him back. You reach out for him, but the next wave throws him back. He disappears. It's all you can do to hang on yourself. "Ben!" you scream, but he doesn't reappear.

It takes all your strength to pull yourself up along the rail. Finally, you reach the deck. Flashes of sharp lightning streak across the dark sky. Wave after wave washes over the deck as everyone frantically tries to keep the boat upright. You can't tell who's who in the driving rain and darkness. There are two people near the tall mast. They're trying to get the sail down.

The storm must have come on fast if the sail was still up when it hit. Two figures move on the other side of the boat, near the area where the lifeboats are stored.

To go to the lifeboats, turn to page 52.

To try to help get the sail down, turn to page 69.

Kat and another diver, Ian, are struggling with an inflatable lifeboat. It's so large that each time they try to get it into the water, the wind pulls it away. You grab one side, and together you manage to get it upright. As you try to drop the boat overboard, a wave washes over the deck. It rips the lifeboat from everyone's grasp. In an instant it's gone.

Ian pulls you to the back of the boat, where a small inflatable raft is usually tied. It's the raft the divers used each day to get out to the coral reefs. There's no way it could still be there in this storm! You're shocked to see it in the water, upside down.

With a sickening screech of wood and metal, the boat begins to tear apart. Ian grabs the rope tethering the raft to the boat and jumps into the water, followed by Kat. You grab the rope and jump too. Somehow you manage not to let go of the rope when you hit the water. Moving hand-over-hand, you reach the raft and cling desperately to the side.

There's someone else in the water near the raft. Ben! Quickly he cuts the rope tying the raft to the sailboat. The raft shoots away on the crest of a wave, carrying all four of you with it.

You keep trying to get the raft upright. But every time, a wave comes and blows it back. Exhausted from battling the waves, you, Ben, Kat, and Ian cling to the raft, treading water and wondering what will happen next.

Turn to page 58.

Night sailing is one of the best things about this trip. You lie on your back on the deck, marveling at the millions of stars in the sky. The gentle rocking motion of the boat lulls you to sleep.

A gust of wind awakens you. Choppy, rough waves rock the boat. A few raindrops are splashing the deck. The stars have disappeared, replaced by a blanket of clouds. It doesn't seem too bad, though. You remind yourself that Andy said there wasn't anything to worry about.

As the waves get rougher, you get more worried. No one is on deck, which means that everyone is likely still asleep. If you wake them and it's nothing, they'll all be angry with you. But if the weather turns bad, everyone will need to be alert.

To let them sleep, go to page 55.

To wake everyone up, turn to page 70.

If the captain isn't worried, you shouldn't be either. But it's getting too rough to stay on deck, so you make your way to your berth. You just settle in when you hear a sudden howl of the wind. The boat pitches hard, throwing you to the floor.

Grabbing your all-weather jacket, you dash out of your cabin. Water is pouring down the ladder. You bang on doors, yelling "Get up!" Kat and Ben are already dressed, but you have to shake Lisa awake. Ian isn't in his cabin.

The water in the boat is almost knee-deep and rising fast. Ben gets to the ladder first and grabs the rail. Then he pulls each of you through the rushing water and up the stairs. As soon as you reach the deck, a huge wave hits the boat. It's all you can do to hang on. Wave after wave throws the boat to one side, then another.

Turn the page.

Someone grabs you and pushes you toward the back of the boat. The small outboard raft the divers use to get to the shallow coral reefs is usually tied up here. It's gone, but you see a flash of white in the water below. It's the raft, swept off the deck and turned upside down.

You don't have time to wonder why there's no proper lifeboat as the sail above catches the wind. The mast twists like a corkscrew and breaks, falling to the deck with a crash of tangled ropes, cloth, and wood. Just before it hits, you jump into the raging ocean and manage to land near the raft. Ben's made it, and so have Kat and Ian. There's no sign of Lisa or Andy.

Ben saws with a small knife at the rope that tethers the raft to the boat. In a few minutes he cuts through the rope. Instantly the raft shoots out on the huge waves. You all try to turn the raft upright, but every time, a wave hits and turns it over again.

Everyone is exhausted from battling the waves and the raft. Finally, you all stop fighting the storm. You cling to the raft and tread water, hoping the storm will end soon.

Ocean storms can include swirling clouds and large waves.

Turn the page.

The storm rages for what seems like hours. But finally it dies down. The ocean calms as the rain tapers off. As the sky lightens with the dawn, you're horrified to see that the sailboat is gone. There isn't any debris on the water, either. Either the storm took everything, or the raft has drifted far away.

Ben and Kat appear to be OK. You've got scrapes and bruises but nothing serious. Everyone is cold and shivering as they cling to the raft. Even though the Caribbean water is about 76 degrees, it's still about 20 degrees lower than normal body temperature. You'll last longer in this water than in cold water before hypothermia sets in, but not that much longer.

Ian seems to be sleeping, so you paddle over and gently shake him.

"Ian, how are you doing?" you ask. He stares at you, confused.

"Legs hurt," he says, and then puts his head back down. You tell the others that you think Ian's really hurt. All of you need to get out of the water.

To try to flip the boat, turn to page 60.

To try to climb on top of the overturned raft, turn to page 72.

The ocean is calm, so there's a good chance you'll be able to get the raft upright. Ben climbs onto the raft and stands up on one side. His body weight forces the other side to rise out of the water like a seesaw. Quickly Kat pushes the raft farther up, and they manage to flip it over. Ben and Kat climb in. They then help you haul Ian into the raft. You climb in last.

The extent of Ian's injuries shocks everyone. He has several deep cuts up and down his legs. Some of the cuts are already red and oozing pus. Red streaks run up his legs. He's got a fever.

"Infection," Ben says. "There's not much we can do." You wrap his cuts with socks and make him comfortable. Then you look around for anything that will keep you alive.

There is a layer of waterproof rubber on the bottom of the boat, which Ben pries off. "We can use this to keep the sun off us," he explains, rigging a makeshift roof over Ian. Everyone checks his or her pockets. You come up with half a bottle of water and some paperclips. Kat has a CD. Ben has his small knife and a half-eaten sandwich in a plastic bag.

"Let's wait," Ben says. "We can live off the water we already have in our bodies for a few hours at least."

The first day you don't do anything but curl up under the rubber roof and try to sleep. You must keep still and quiet to conserve energy. The sun is merciless. You and the others dip your clothing in the ocean and put it back on. You know this will help keep your body cool and avoid heatstroke. But you must make sure that everything is dry before the night brings colder temperatures.

Turn the page.

Ian is burning with fever and unresponsive. By morning he's dead. The three of you remove his clothes and gently slide his body into the sea. His pockets were empty, but all of you wash the blood and pus out of his clothing and divide it among you.

By now you're thirsty and starving, but no one wants to eat or drink yet. "Maybe we can catch some fish," you say, pulling a paper clip out of your pocket. You bend it into a hook and then unravel some of the thread from your shirt for a line.

"Don't handle the fishing line with your bare hands, and don't wrap it around your hands—it can cut you," Ben says, tearing off a small piece of the bread from his sandwich for bait. Nodding, you slip off your shirt and wrap it around your hand. Crossing your fingers, you lower your fishing line into the water.

Almost immediately you get a hit! You pull up a strange-looking fish with spots on its body and big, round eyes. Its face looks like a toad.

Some species of porcupine puffer fish are deadly to eat.

To eat the fish, turn to page **64**.

To throw it back and try again, turn to page **65**.

You're so hungry and thirsty that you can barely wait for Ben to slice the fish open before you start eating. It takes about half an hour before your mouth begins to tingle. You get so dizzy that you collapse, then vomit. Ben and Kat vomit over the side of the raft and start gasping for air. Your chest feels tight. It's hard to breathe. Your arms and legs start to go numb too.

You vaguely remember something about puffer fish being very poisonous. The toxin in their bodies causes paralysis and death. So that must be what this strange fish was. But it's too late now. The tightness in your chest gets worse, but you pass out before your heart stops beating.

THE END

To follow another path, turn to page 13.
To read the conclusion, turn to page 105.

It looks like a puffer fish, which are poisonous unless prepared carefully. You sigh and throw it back. The next time, you pull up a fish that looks more normal. None of you recognize it.

"Well," says Kat, "It's doesn't have pale, shiny gills or flabby skin. It doesn't smell bad. I guess it's OK to eat." The three of you tear into it, eating it raw. Ben breaks the spine and you suck the fresh liquid out of the bones. You even eat a fish eye, which is a great source of water.

You pull off small bits of fish for bait. After an hour or so, you have several more fish lying in the raft. Ben slices the few remaining pieces of fish and lays them out to dry. You'll use them for food and bait tomorrow.

Turn the page.

"I wonder where we are," you say. You see a group of sea birds flying in the distance. Ben sees them too. Then you both notice seaweed floating in the water.

"Hey, we must be close to land," Ben says excitedly. "Birds and seaweed are clues." You grab as much seaweed as you can reach. Seaweed is a warm covering—plus, you can eat it.

"We could follow the birds," Kat says. "We can paddle the boat with our hands and take turns swimming and pulling the raft."

To take turns pulling the raft, go to page 67.

To stay on the raft, turn to page 75.

If there are birds and seaweed, land can't be too far away. You all watch the birds for a while, and you think you've figured out what direction they are flying from. That's where the land must be.

"I'm the strongest swimmer," Ben says. He ties the frayed raft rope around his waist and starts swimming in the direction of the birds. You take turns through the day pulling the raft until you see a small island far in the distance. You can't believe it!

As you get closer, you see white-capped waves crash against the shoreline. It doesn't look quite right, but you're exhausted. The fading light and your hunger must be playing tricks on your eyes.

To try to land here, turn to page 77.

To look for a beach, turn to page 78.

It'll only take a few seconds to grab your passport, some water, and some extra clothing. As you're digging through your duffle bag, the boat rocks sharply to the left. It sends you flying against the wall. Something in your arm pops, and a sharp pain sears through your shoulder. Screaming, you drop to your knees in the water. The roar of the ocean means the storm is hitting full force. You've got to move!

Painfully, you get up and stumble through the door toward the steep ladder to the deck. Before you reach it, a roar of ocean water cascades down the stairs and throws you backward. The last thing you see is the darkness of the sea as it covers you.

THE END

To follow another path, turn to page 13.
To read the conclusion, turn to page 105.

You slip and slide to the mast, hanging onto whatever you can to keep from going overboard. Andy and Lisa, another passenger, are there. The three of you pull at the sail, but it's no use. The winds are too strong. The sail billows outward in the wind, taking a tangle of ropes with it. The rope you're holding quickly knots around your legs.

As the sail whips out into the sea, it pulls you with it. You gasp as the heavy mast hits you in the chest. You're flung into the water, limp and lifeless.

THE END

To follow another path, turn to page 13.
To read the conclusion, turn to page 105.

Sure enough, everyone is angry with you for waking them. They're upset until Andy appears, holding a piece of paper.

"The storm has changed course," he says gravely. "Get on deck—I need everyone's help."

You've no sooner reached the deck than the storm hits. The light rain transforms into a raging downpour as huge waves rise and crash over the deck. The sail billows and twists crazily in the wind. Then the tall mast snaps, throwing sails, rope, and wood into the storm.

Everyone gets to the lifeboat. It takes every hand to get it upright and into the water. You all scramble aboard. The lifeboat rises and falls on the huge waves, and you vomit several times. But you're alive. You all huddle under the boat's plastic canopy, trying to stay as dry as possible. Eventually the wind dies down. The rain slows and then stops. You peek out from under the canopy.

The sky is getting lighter, so sunrise is near. There's no sign of the sailboat, not even any debris. It's a good thing you woke everyone up when you did. If you'd delayed only a few minutes, you all might be dead now.

The lifeboat is well stocked with emergency supplies. You pop a seasickness pill under your tongue and drink a bit of water. Andy shoots an emergency flare, followed by another a few minutes later. By midmorning a Coast Guard boat appears on the horizon. Your vacation might have been ruined, but now you can tell stories about surviving a storm at sea.

THE END

To follow another path, turn to page 13.
To read the conclusion, turn to page 105.

The three of you hoist Ian onto the raft. When his legs clear the water, you're shocked. Several deep gashes crisscross his calves and feet. A couple of them are red and oozing pus. Kat removes one of her socks and ties it around a wound. You and Ben do the same. It's not enough, but it's all you can do.

"Come on, we all need to get up there," Ben says, hauling himself onto the raft. But when you and Kat try to join him, the weight of all of you swamps the small raft. You and Ben quickly slide into the water.

For the next several hours you, Ben, and Kat take turns climbing onto the raft. Ian stays there, but he's developed a raging fever. He tosses and turns, muttering things that make no sense. You do what you can to make him comfortable, but he never regains consciousness. The next morning, you find that he's died. You and the others gently slide his body into the ocean.

It's your turn to be in the water. You put your jacket over your head to block the blazing sun. You doze off, but are awakened by something bumping your leg.

You try not to scream. The water is filled with sharks! You stop treading water and let your body float. Maybe the sharks won't bother you.

Blood in the water can provoke a shark attack.

Turn the page.

You stay as still as possible, letting your body float free. Ben and Kat slowly pull you up about halfway onto the overturned raft. It's all the weight the raft can handle, but you're grateful. Now you're only exposed to the sharks from your thighs down.

Closing your eyes, you try not to think about the circling sharks. Every now and then, something bumps your feet. Staying still is the hardest thing you've ever done. After about an hour, the sharks swim away.

As the sun begins to set, you hear the sound of a helicopter. Kat and Ben yell and wave their hands, but you don't have the strength to move. Suddenly there's a splash, and a man in an orange rescue suit is beside you. You and your friends are saved.

THE END

To follow another path, turn to page 13.
To read the conclusion, turn to page 105.

"We have no idea where land is," you argue. "Besides, we know we can survive on this raft. It'll only be a matter of time before someone finds us."

It's getting hot, so you all crawl under the rubber roof. You cover your exposed skin with wet seaweed and fall asleep immediately.

When you awake it's late afternoon. The others are still asleep. You stretch, trying to ignore your sunburned skin and the sea salt blisters on your hands and face. Looking up, you wonder if the birds are still here. Sure enough, you see one in the distance. But it's not a bird. It's a small airplane!

You dive for Kat's jacket and pull out the CD. Using it like mirror, you angle it until it reflects toward the airplane. Frantically you flick the CD back and forth, hoping the pilot will see the signal. At first you don't think the plane sees you. Then it roars overhead, dipping its wings back and forth. Yes! It flies away, but you know it saw you.

An hour later a Coast Guard boat appears. You, Ben, and Kat start cheering. Rescued at last! You only wish that Ian could have made it too.

A Dutch Coast Guard boat braves a storm to rescue stranded sailors.

THE END

To follow another path, turn to page 13.
To read the conclusion, turn to page 105.

Excitedly you all jump in the water and make the final push for land. The current tugs you, and then carries you forward with surprising strength. As you approach, the white-capped waves seem bigger and louder, and they're breaking farther from shore than you thought. It's not until you're on top of them that you realize that the waves are crashing against a line of sharp, deadly coral.

Before any of you can get away, the current pushes you into the small reef. The raft is sliced into shreds, and you feel as if a hundred knives are cutting you. The waves push you again, raking you over the coral reef and carrying you to the tiny shore beyond. You lay there, growing weaker as blood pours from the cuts. You made the wrong decision, and now it's going to cost you your life.

THE END

To follow another path, turn to page 13.
To read the conclusion, turn to page 105.

"I don't like the look of those waves," says Kat. "There might be rocks or coral there, which would slice us into a million pieces."

You turn the raft toward the end of the island and keep paddling. Finally, you spot a small white beach and aim for it. As you get closer, you see several figures appear out of the palm trees beyond the beach. They run into the surf and pull you to land. You lay on the warm sand, gasping and heaving, so relieved to be out of the water that you can't speak.

Your rescuers take the three of you to a large house nearby and give you food, water, and first aid. You tell them all about the storm, the accident, and your ordeal.

"Where are we?" you finally manage to ask.

Small islands dot much of the world's oceans.

"It's a privately owned island," one of the men responds. "Don't worry," he adds kindly. "You and your friends are safe now."

THE END

To follow another path, turn to page 13.
To read the conclusion, turn to page 105.

Some anglers use speedboats to fish in the ocean.

CHAPTER 4

Alone in the Ocean

There's nothing you love more than to take your dad's small motorboat out for a day of fishing off the coast of Maine, where your family is vacationing. Most of the time you like to fish with friends, but today you're thinking of going out alone.

You're an experienced boater and angler, but you've never gone out solo before. It's kind of exciting to think about being by yourself for a few hours. When you gather your fishing gear, you also remember to take some supplies. You pack sandwiches, fruit, and cookies in a cooler, along with a gallon of water. You bring a small radio to monitor the weather, a waterproof flashlight, and a flare gun.

Turn the page.

To be on the safe side, you grab an extra life jacket and an emergency thermal blanket. Just as you're going out the door, you spy some rope and toss that in as well.

In the boat are seat cushions, a plastic jug of gas, and a toolbox. The gas tank gauge says full, the anchor is securely connected to the rope, and everything is ready to go. You're out on the water before dawn. There are a couple of places you like to fish. One is only a few miles offshore. The better one is an hour's boat trip into the open ocean.

To stay close to land, go to page **83.**

To go out to sea, turn to page **84.**

You go just beyond the sight of land and anchor the boat. As the sun rises, you drop your line. The fish don't seem to be biting this morning. You love being on the water, so you don't mind. As the day wears on, the sky fills with clouds and the water becomes choppy. Flipping on the radio, you hear a weather report of a small storm. This doesn't worry you. Small, quick storms blow through all the time.

About noon, the fish start biting furiously. Most of them are too small to keep, so you spend most of your time throwing them back.

By late afternoon the clouds above have gotten darker, the wind has picked up, and the boat is bobbing furiously on the choppy water. But the weather report says the storm is passing to the east. You should be safe, but those clouds don't look good.

To fish some more, turn to page 85.

To go back in, turn to page 95.

The sun is just over the horizon when you reach your favorite fishing area. It doesn't disappoint you. In a couple of hours you have an impressive number of large fish.

As you unwrap a sandwich and open a soda, you remember another great fishing spot your uncle told you about. It's another hour out, though. Glancing at the sky, you see dark clouds in the distance. All you can get from the radio is static because you're too far out for a weather report. The last forecast you heard said it would be cloudy with some small storms. That shouldn't be anything to worry about.

To go farther out to sea, turn to page 87.

To stay put, turn to page 97.

The sky looks clearer to the north. Maybe you can get around the storm by heading that way. You yank on the anchor, but it's stuck on something. You pull until your arms hurt, but the anchor isn't budging. You could cut the rope, but then you'd lose the anchor. Maybe you can pull it up with the boat. The motor revs up instantly and the boat zooms forward. The front of the boat rises in the air, pulling the anchor rope tight. Quickly you shut off the motor, but it's too late. The rope snaps and the boat flips over, sending you and all your supplies into the ocean.

The water is freezing! You come up, sputtering. The waves and wind are getting stronger, and the sky is darkening. With a sickening feeling you realize that everyone was asleep when you left this morning. No one knows where you are.

Turn the page.

If you can get the boat upright, you may be able to get home. But the waves are so strong there's no guarantee that you can do that.

Small boats can flip and capsize easily during storms.

To stay in the water with the boat, turn to page 89.

To try to flip the boat over, turn to page 96.

You imagine the huge fish you'll catch in the new spot as the boat moves through the rough waves. It takes longer to get there than you thought. You drop your line, but the storm clouds are moving closer, and the waves kick up. A gust of chilly wind hits you. This was a bad idea. Stashing your gear, you turn for home, hoping to outrun the storm.

About 20 minutes later, the outboard motor sputters and chokes, then dies. The waves are much stronger and water is washing over the side of the boat. Frantically you check the motor and discover you're out of gas. Relief floods you as you grab the plastic gas jug. But the jug feels light, and it takes only a minute to see it's almost empty. You're sick to your stomach as you realize you didn't check it. You assumed the tank was full, so you didn't bother. You hurriedly pour the gas into the tank and continue on, even though you know you won't make it.

Turn the page.

Sure enough, the motor chokes and dies again. The wind is really strong now, and the waves toss the boat around like a bathtub toy. A huge wave catches you and sends you into the water. Another wave hits the boat and flips it over. Desperately you grab the boat and hang on.

The waves batter you and the overturned boat for what seems like hours. Then as fast as it appeared, the storm moves away. The sun comes out, and you're shocked to see that it's late afternoon. The storm only lasted an hour! You haven't been in the water as long as you thought. That makes your chance of survival much better.

The first thing to do is gather any supplies you can find. A few things are floating near the boat. But the waves are still strong, so you only have time to grab a few items before they're all washed out of reach. Once you have some supplies, then you can figure out what to do next.

To choose the seat cushion, the gas jug, and the thermal blanket, turn to page 90.

To grab the cooler, the rope, and the waterproof flashlight, turn to page 93.

You've lost the life jacket, but shoving the seat cushion under your jacket and zipping it up keeps you afloat. Using the thermal blanket, you tie the gas can to the boat, so it can't float away. You're too exhausted to try to get the boat upright. But you manage to climb on top of it. Now if you only had something to eat or drink.

The sunset is so beautiful that it almost makes you forget your dangerous situation. When the sun is down, the temperature turns much colder. The water is still choppy, and it takes all your strength to hang onto the boat. But you don't dare get back in the water and risk hypothermia.

Around midnight more storm clouds come, and the rain starts. Opening your mouth to catch it, you only manage to get a few drops. You need more.

To use the thermal blanket, go to page 91.

To catch rainwater with the gas can, turn to page 98.

Quickly you rinse out the jug with seawater. The thermal blanket is made from Mylar, a silver polyester substance. You roll it into a makeshift funnel. You stick the small end of the funnel into the jug. Immediately rainwater cascades into the jug. It works! By the time the rain stops, the jug is more than half full. That's enough water to keep you alive for several days, if needed.

At dawn you make more plans. Tearing a narrow strip from the thermal blanket, you tie the jug securely to the boat. A second strip of blanket will be a signal flag. You stretch the rest of the silver metallic thermal blanket over the boat. The sun is beating down, so you wet your clothing and put it all back on to keep your body temperature down. You crawl under the blanket, using the seat cushion as a pillow. Every time you wake up, you stand on the boat and wave the signal flag.

Turn the page.

At sunrise you're dizzy and desperately hungry. The cooler is long gone, but maybe there's something else to eat trapped under the boat. It might be safer to stay on the boat, though.

A thermal blanket works by deflecting body heat back to the source.

To stay on the boat, turn to page **99**.

To dive under and search for food, turn to page **100**.

Dropping the flashlight into the cooler, you tie the rope through the handle. You then strap it to the boat. There's a chance that you can turn the boat upright. For a time you watch the waves to see what direction they're moving. Then you push the boat so that it sits perpendicular to the direction of the waves. When you stand on one side and pull upward, the force of the waves pushes the boat even farther. It takes a few tries, but finally the boat is upright. You climb aboard and pull the cooler in with you.

No one knows where you are, you realize suddenly. Trying not to panic, you take stock of your situation. There's enough food and drinks to last a few days, if you ration it carefully. The boat seems to be in good shape. The flashlight is useless unless you need to signal at night. Halfheartedly you try the motor. As expected, it's not working.

Turn the page.

The sun is setting, and a gust of cool wind reminds you how cold it can get on the ocean after dark. With no blankets or coverings, all you can do is curl up in the bottom of the boat and stay out of the wind. It's too cold to get much sleep, but you manage to survive the night. For the next two days you sleep, eat and drink as little as possible, and scan the ocean and sky for signs of rescue. But you're alone.

By the fourth day your supplies are almost gone. You've seen several schools of fish swimming under the boat. But they're swimming too deep to catch. There must be something on the boat you can use to catch fish.

To try to make a hook, turn to page 102.

To try to make a net, turn to page 103.

The weather can be unpredictable, and you're not taking any chances. Just as you stash your fishing gear and start the motor, a huge wave hits the boat. You're almost thrown into the water, but manage to hang on. That was too close. The anchor seems to be caught on something, but a few tugs and it's free. Opening the engine full throttle, you speed for home.

The waves batter your boat. It's all you can do to bail out the water and keep moving in the right direction. The sky grows darker and the waves get stronger, but your little boat manages to stay on top of them. Finally you see land. You won't have any big fish to brag about, but at least you're alive.

THE END

To follow another path, turn to page 13.
To read the conclusion, turn to page 105.

You know how to flip a boat—get on top of it and stand on one edge, while pulling the other side up with a rope or a handle. Climbing onto the overturned boat is easy, but the waves and wind keep knocking the boat down.

Panicking, you keep trying. The sky grows darker, and flashes of lightning cut the sky above you. Sobbing in frustration and fear, you try again. But this time the wind catches the boat and hurls it sideways, hitting your head and knocking you into the water. You're unconscious as you slide under the waves.

THE END

To follow another path, turn to page 13.
To read the conclusion, turn to page 105.

Those clouds don't look good, but you have another couple of hours before you need to head for home. You're so intent on catching a big fish that you don't notice the sky darkening or that the waves are getting very rough. When a cold wave splashes into the boat, you realize what's happening. Quickly you store your gear and turn for home. From the look of those clouds, it's going to be close.

The waves get bigger and cold wind whips through you, but the boat stays afloat as you keep it pointed toward home. Just as the storm clouds open with torrents of rain, you reach the shore. Your dad is standing on the beach in the pouring rain, waving his arms at you. You've never been so glad to see someone in your life.

THE END

To follow another path, turn to page 13.
To read the conclusion, turn to page 105.

The gas can, of course! You rinse it out with seawater and then hold it up into the rain. By the time the rain stops you have about an inch of water in the jug.

By noon the next day you've drank all the water. No rain clouds are in sight. You slip into the water to cool off. You're so tired that you don't bother climbing back. But you've got to be out of the water and dry before nightfall. You pull the thermal blanket over your head and drift off to sleep.

When you wake up, the stars are out. There's a chilly wind blowing. Your mind feels sluggish and dull. The water is much warmer than the cold air. You can't remember why it was so important to get on the boat last night. You drift off to sleep again. You're dreaming of taking a warm bath as you sink below the surface of the water and drown.

THE END

To follow another path, turn to page 13.
To read the conclusion, turn to page 105.

Rescue crews use inflatable boats to search for shipwreck survivors.

You have to stay on the boat. Swallowing the last of the fresh water, you sit up and cover yourself with the thermal blanket. Every now and then you wave the signal flag. You pound on the boat, kick your legs—anything you can think of to keep moving and alert. You sing every song you remember, even the ABC song. When you hear the sound of a helicopter, you think you're hearing things. It's not until a man in an orange suit jumps into the water that you realize rescue has come.

THE END

To follow another path, turn to page 13.
To read the conclusion, turn to page 105.

The water is dark under the boat, and the first search turns up empty. On the third try, you find a plastic bag with your sandwich, fruit, and cookies. You eat the sandwich and wash it down with the rest of the water.

You decide to stay in the water through the heat of the day. A gust of wind blows the thermal blanket away from the boat. You reach for it but miss. It floats away. You lean against the side of the boat and doze off and on until the sun sets.

When you wake, it's hard to think clearly. You remember that you must get out of the water.

Painfully you climb back onto the hull of the boat. It's freezing up here, and your soaked clothing makes it feel even colder. First you start shaking, but eventually that stops. Suddenly you have the urge to play basketball with your brother.

Hypothermia Chart

If the Water Temp. (F) is...	Exhaustion or Unconsciousness Sets In	Expected Time of Survival Is...
32.5	Less than 15 min.	Less than 15–45 min.
32.5–40	15–30 min.	30–90 min.
40–50	30–60 min.	1–3 hours
50–60	1–2 hours	1–6 hours
60–70	2–7 hours	2–40 hours
70–80	3–12 hours	3 hrs–indefinitely
more than 80	indefinitely	indefinitely

"Well, this is no place for some hoops," you think as you peel off your clothing. You're so far gone with hypothermia that you don't realize what you're doing. You dive into the water and start swimming for home. Of course, you never arrive.

THE END

To follow another path, turn to page 13.
To read the conclusion, turn to page 105.

After a few minutes of tinkering, you have a small pile of wires, springs, and coils. You bend a wire into a large hook and pull some strands out of the rope to use as a fishing line. Two cookies are left in the cooler. You use a piece of a cookie for bait.

For the next few hours you try to fish. It's becoming hard to concentrate, so you give up. You drink the last of the water and eat the remaining cookies.

By nightfall you are dizzy, disoriented, and so thirsty. Surely drinking a little seawater won't hurt. By morning, the vomiting starts. Somewhere in your dehydrated brain, you get the idea to fill the cooler up with saltwater and try to turn it into fresh water. You throw the cooler into the ocean and jump in after it. It's the last decision you ever make.

THE END

To follow another path, turn to page 13.
To read the conclusion, turn to page 105.

You tear your T-shirt open to form a large rectangle. Then you tie the corners together to one end of the rope. You lower it in the water and wait. A flash of silver means a school of fish has arrived. You pull your makeshift net through the fish. Finally you get the hang of it, throwing several small, flopping fish into the boat. You use a piece of wire from the motor to clean one of the fish and eat greedily. The eyes are good sources of liquid. You're so thirsty that eating them doesn't seem gross.

As it gets dark, you switch on the flashlight and shine it upward. Switching off the flashlight, you curl up in the boat and drift off. When the shaking starts, you try to push it away. It gets stronger, and you open your eyes. Someone has you by the shoulders. Then a woman's voice cuts through your foggy brain. "We saw your signal." You're rescued!

THE END

To follow another path, turn to page 13.
To read the conclusion, turn to page 105.

Severe storms can come up suddenly on the ocean.

CHAPTER 5

You CAN Survive

Water covers 75 percent of Earth's surface, and about 70 percent of that is ocean or sea. Most people will find themselves traveling on or above the water at some point in their lives. There is always the possibility that something might go wrong. Survival depends on your resourcefulness and ability to think and act quickly and rationally.

Most deaths at sea come from making bad choices and forgetting how powerful and dangerous the sea can be. The best way to survive is to keep your wits and to think clearly about what you're facing. Making the right decisions in the first minutes you're stranded in the water can mean the difference between living and dying. Knowing that most people lost at sea die of hypothermia, dehydration, or starvation is vital.

Even if you're just on the boat as a passenger, taking a sailing safety class before you go out on the water is a good idea. Then you'll be more prepared and less likely to panic during an emergency.

Being clear-headed about your immediate situation will keep you alive. You must be able to judge when to leave a boat in trouble, and when it's safer to ride out a storm. Get familiar with the boat. Where are the lifeboats and life jackets stored? Can you get to emergency supplies quickly? Can you radio for help?

If the worst happens and you find yourself lost at sea, you must remain calm and focused on staying alive. Is anyone injured? Do you have food and water? Are there other dangers nearby, such as sharks or coral reefs? Does anyone know where you are? Are you near land? The faster you understand the dangers you're facing, the better able you are to make a plan for survival.

Ultimately it's your will to live that will help you survive being lost at sea. If you focus on staying alive and not giving up, you have a much better chance of living through your ordeal.

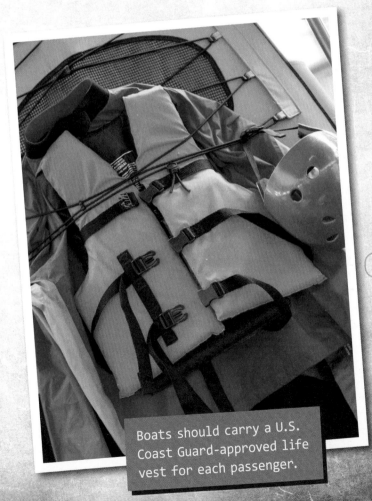

Boats should carry a U.S. Coast Guard-approved life vest for each passenger.

REAL SURVIVORS

Yacht Wreck

Maurice and Maralyn Bailey's sea ordeal began when they set sail from Southampton, England, on their way to New Zealand. They sailed safely for several months until a whale destroyed their 31-foot yacht in March 1973. They salvaged some food, water, and supplies and escaped in a life raft. When the food ran out, they survived on rainwater and fish they caught using a bent safety pin. By the time they were rescued by a Korean fishing boat June 30, 1973, their clothing had rotted away, they had each lost about 40 pounds, and the lifeboat was falling apart.

Adrift in a Lifeboat

Steve Callahan was an experienced sailor and boat builder when he left Rhode Island on his small ship, bound for Antigua. In January 1982 his boat was severely damaged in a storm in the Atlantic Ocean. He managed to get onto a lifeboat with a sleeping bag and an emergency kit with food, flares, a spear gun, and solar stills that could produce water. He survived by eating fish, barnacles, and birds. When fishermen found him April 20, 1982, near the Caribbean island of Marie-Galante, he was dehydrated and covered with saltwater sores, but alive.

A Dangerous Swim

Late one September afternoon in 2008, Walt Marino and his 12-year-old son Christopher waded out to swim near Daytona Beach, Florida. They were caught in a riptide that carried them both out to sea. They survived by treading water, but after several hours the two were separated. As night fell, they stayed in contact by shouting "To infinity and beyond!" from the movie *Toy Story*. Fishermen rescued Walt the next morning. Christopher was found alive a few hours later.

Lost in a Dinghy

Three teenage boys set sail the night of October 5, 2010, from their South Pacific island home and ended up lost at sea for 50 days. The three boys, Filo Filo and Samuel Pelesa, 15, and Edward Nasau, 14, decided to sail from Atafu Atoll to an island 60 miles away. They collected coconuts and set out, but their 12-foot metal dinghy's motor eventually lost power, and they drifted out to sea. After the coconuts ran out, they drank rainwater they caught in a tarp and ate fish and birds. A fishing boat near Fiji—more than 750 miles away from their home—finally rescued them.

SURVIVAL QUIZ

You're in the middle of the ocean on a small sailboat when a storm hits. There's a lot of equipment on board, but you only have time to grab a few things before you get into the lifeboat. Which items will help you survive being lost at sea? Rank each of these items 1-10, from life saving to totally worthless.

A. compass
B. nylon rope
C. extra water
D. case of freeze-dried food
E. floating seat cushion
F. ocean maps
G. fishing kit
H. case of chocolate bars
I. square plastic tarp
J. shaving mirror

Source: Training Manager Success Strategies

Answers: C, J, D, I, H, G, B, E, F, A

Can You Survive

ANTARCTICA?

An Interactive Survival Adventure

by Rachael Hanel

Consultant:
John Splettstoesser
International Association of Antarctica Tour Operators
Waconia, Minnesota

TABLE OF CONTENTS

About Your
ADVENTURE

YOU are traveling through the bleakest, coldest place on Earth—Antarctica. This place is like nothing you have ever experienced.

In this book you'll deal with extreme survival situations. You'll explore how the knowledge you have and the choices you make can mean the difference between life and death.

Chapter One sets the scene. Then you choose which path to read. Follow the directions at the bottom of each page. The choices you make will change your outcome. After you finish one path, go back and read the others for new perspectives and more adventures.

YOU CHOOSE the path you take through your adventure.

Antarctica is considered a desert, even though it is covered with ice.

CHAPTER 1

The Last Place on Earth

Few places on Earth are as unforgiving, dangerous, and cold as Antarctica. Average summer temperatures on this continent that surrounds the South Pole are just 20 degrees Fahrenheit. The average winter temperature is -30 F and can plunge as low as -100 F. Raging blizzards seem to come out of nowhere.

Yet people have regularly traveled to Antarctica since the early 1900s. In the early days, adventurous men scrambled onto its icy surface to explore the unknown land. Later scientists went to the continent to learn more about weather, geology, and global warming.

Turn the page.

Adventurous travelers journey to Antarctica on cruise ships.

Today scientists and other workers live at the many research stations scattered about the continent. Even casual travelers board cruise ships that stop at Antarctica's shores.

Almost all travel to Antarctica takes place during its summer months, which are November to February. The cold and near-constant dark of the Antarctic winter make it difficult for humans to survive.

But dangers lurk all around even in summer. Snowstorms or just an overcast sky can make it impossible to see in front of you. What seems to be a clear path may hold hidden dangers, such as deep crevasses in the ice. The intensity of the sun's rays reflected off the snow can burn the corneas of the eyes, causing snow blindness.

Those traveling even for short periods outside may become victims of frostbite and hypothermia. Frostbite often occurs in fingers, feet, ears, and the nose. If it is not treated quickly, it destroys skin and tissue. Hypothermia, which occurs when the body's temperature gets too low, is often deadly.

Antarctica's isolation and remoteness can breed danger. No hospitals exist. Many research stations do have medical doctors. But if you aren't near a research station, it can take a long time to get help. Even something as simple as a toothache can become a serious problem.

Turn the page.

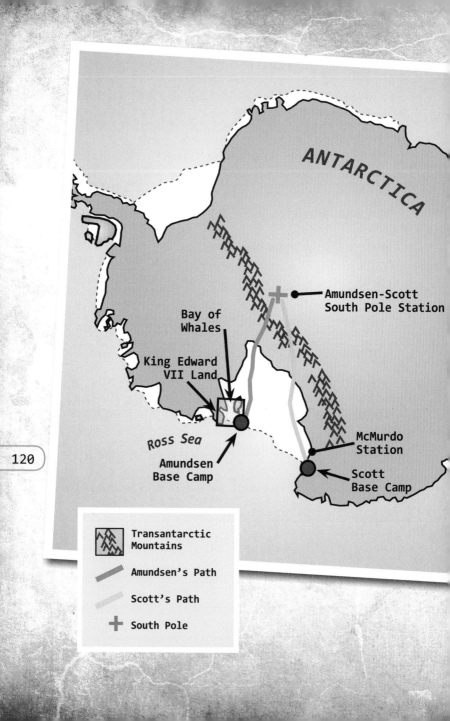

ANTARCTICA

Amundsen-Scott
South Pole Station

Bay of
Whales

King Edward
VII Land

Ross *Sea*

Amundsen
Base Camp

McMurdo
Station

Scott
Base Camp

120

Transantarctic
Mountains

Amundsen's Path

Scott's Path

South Pole

Anyone who plans to travel to or work in Antarctica must be smart and well prepared. Trips are sometimes planned years in advance. You travel by airplane to somewhere near Antarctica, such as Australia, Argentina, or New Zealand. Then you board a small cargo plane to the Antarctic coast. Weather conditions must be perfect in order to land.

When it is time to leave, you must be sure you are ready. After February no more planes can come or go because of the darkness and cold.

Your body and mind will be put to the test on your Antarctic adventure. Your survival depends on the choices you make. It is your job to travel to Antarctica and make it home alive. Will you be able to do it?

To test your skills as an early Antarctic explorer, turn to page 123.

To travel the continent as a modern-day adventurer, turn to page 155.

To live and work in Antarctica in modern times, turn to page 183.

Roald Amundsen began his expedition to the South Pole in 1911.

CHAPTER 2

Race to the Pole

The year is 1911. Many parts of the world still remain mostly untouched by humans. Adventurous people seek out these unexplored areas. They want to be the first to set foot on a new land.

Two teams of explorers are each quietly making plans to be the first to the South Pole. You have a chance to be on one of the teams. The South Pole is a bitterly cold and empty place. No people have ever lived there. The adventure could easily turn deadly. But reaching the South Pole first will bring fame and honor.

You must first decide what expedition you want to join. Roald Amundsen of Norway leads one team. Robert Falcon Scott of Great Britain leads the other.

123

Turn the page.

Scott loaded much of his team's gear on motorized sleds.

Amundsen's team is using skis and 115 sled dogs to travel. Scott is traveling using 19 Siberian ponies and 33 sled dogs. Scott's team also has a new invention—motorized snow sleds.

Scott is more familiar with the Antarctic terrain. He had first tried to reach the South Pole in 1902. But Amundsen is a more experienced polar explorer. He has spent much time in far northern Canada with Inuit villagers. He learned their ways of survival.

Which team do you think has the better chance to reach the South Pole first and survive the return journey?

To be a part of Amundsen's team, turn to page 126.

To go with Scott, turn to page 128.

You and the other members of Amundsen's team started this trip in October 1910. Beginning in February 1911, you place three supply depots along the beginning part of your route. Each depot contains about 2,000 pounds of food and fuel. The depots look like snow towers with the supplies tucked inside. A flag is placed on the top.

The depots are all in place by the end of March. You wait at Framheim, the base camp near the Bay of Whales, through the cold, dark, Antarctic winter. In September 1911 Amundsen is ready to start the journey. But you think September is too soon to start. Still, you leave with Amundsen and six others on September 8, 1911.

The weather quickly turns ugly. Temperatures fall, and the wind picks up. The dogs' frostbitten feet make running painful. Just four days after starting, Amundsen decides to head back to Framheim and wait for better weather.

By September 15 you are just 40 miles from Framheim. But the numbing cold causes you and two other men to get frostbite in your feet. The tingling sensation sends ripples of pain through your body.

Amundsen takes off with two other men. He leaves the rest of you behind because the frostbite has slowed you down. You and the others are left out in the bitter cold with no food or fuel. You use the whip to keep your exhausted dogs going.

Soon after midnight on September 16, you and another teammate struggle into camp. Everyone else made it back hours before. You are angry. Amundsen's decision could have cost you your lives. You want to say something to Amundsen so he doesn't make the same mistake again.

To speak out, turn to page **132**.

To keep quiet, turn to page **134**.

You and the other Scott team members spend early 1911 laying down supplies such as food and fuel along the beginning of your route. You build depots out of the snow as high as you can, with the supplies inside of them.

But your team runs into problems. The motor sleds fail to perform in the cold weather. The Siberian ponies sink to their knees in the soft snow. Seven ponies die from exhaustion or accidents. You can't make it to the last depot location.

Supply depots (center) were placed along the expedition routes.

You leave the base camp at Cape Evans on November 1, 1911. Scott hopes for warmer weather by starting later in the Antarctic spring. He believes the ponies can travel farther in warmer temperatures.

The journey starts poorly. It snows heavily. Then warmer temperatures arrive, and the snow thaws. The soft, wet snow is difficult to trudge through. The remaining ponies are struggling to move. In early December they must be shot because they are slowing down the entire team.

There isn't enough food for everyone to make the journey to the pole. After the ponies are shot, Scott sends the dogs back to the base camp with some of the men. You will be pulling your sled and its 200-pound load yourself.

Turn the page.

On December 10 you reach the Beardmore Glacier. You pause for a moment to look at the task ahead of you.

The trek up the glacier takes all the energy you have. You struggle to lift one foot in front of the other in the deep snow. The winds swirl so much snow you can barely see. When the sun comes out, the glare off the snow causes you to become snow blind. You must rest every few minutes just to catch your breath. Some days you only travel half a mile.

On December 20 Scott sends four men back to base camp. You're relieved not to be among them. You still have a chance to reach the Pole.

After more than two weeks, you finally reach the top of the glacier. Now it's a flat journey to the Pole. You hope it will be easier.

With just 180 miles to go, Scott decides to send back four more men. The sleds are lighter now, and there isn't enough food for eight men. Heading back now might save your life. But you also are eager for the glory that would come with being the first to the South Pole.

To keep going, turn to page 136.

To turn back, turn to page 142.

At breakfast the next morning, you confront Amundsen. "You are the team's leader," you tell him. "It is unthinkable that you left men behind. We nearly died. When we start again, you will have to make sure you take care of all of your men."

Silence fills the room. When Amundsen finally speaks, he is angry.

"I will not tolerate my men telling me what to do," he says. "I know what is best for us." He takes you aside. "I do not want you going with me to the Pole."

Your stomach drops. Amundsen says he is
sending you in a smaller party to explore King Edward VII Land, a peninsula about 800 miles from the Pole. You'll bring two other men with you.

Your group sets forth around the same time Amundsen and four others go toward the South Pole. On the peninsula, you collect rocks and take photos. But toward the end of your journey, a fierce snowstorm strands you for several days. As a result, your supplies of food and fuel are running low. But you still have more exploring to do.

"I think we should head back," you tell your companions. "We have barely enough supplies to last a week. If we leave now, we can return to base camp before the supplies run out."

Turn to page 145.

At breakfast the next morning, you keep quiet. Someone else at your table speaks up. As he listens, Amundsen's face reddens with anger.

"I don't need critics like you on the trip to the Pole," he tells the man. "I will find another job for you."

Amundsen sends him to explore King Edward VII Land. This peninsula is about 800 miles from the South Pole. It is an interesting journey, but not as historic as your journey to the Pole.

You and three other men are going with Amundsen to the Pole. Amundsen calls a meeting. "I need both dogsled drivers and skiers," he says.

A dogsled driver stands on a sled behind a dog team that is pulling the supplies. It is his job to make sure the dogs go where they are supposed to go.

A skier gets to travel lightly. He will go ahead and decide on the right path for the dogsleds.

"Both jobs require much responsibility. I want you to decide which you think will better suit you and the team," Amundsen says.

You are a good skier, and you are also good with dogs. What should you do?

To be a skier, turn to page **138.**

To be a dogsled driver, turn to page **140.**

Scott planned to take just three men with him. But at the last minute, he decides to bring you along for extra pulling power.

But Scott didn't plan for five people on this last leg of the journey. You're short one pair of skis, and Scott's tent only sleeps four. You're worried that you will run out of supplies. Five men use more food and fuel than four men.

You forget about those problems as you get closer to the Pole. You're almost there! As you get closer, you see something in the distance. It's a scrap of cloth tied to a pole.

"Could it be?" you ask Scott quietly. "Could the Norwegians have beaten us?"

You arrive at the Pole and see the Norwegian flag. Your suspicions are correct.

"We are not the first," Scott says sadly. "But we have made it. You all have done a good job."

You spend two days there. With a heavy heart, you start the return journey. The winds howl. The snow and ice cut into your face. One day you are not dressed properly for the sudden storm that appears. Your clothes are soaked.

Scott's team found Amundsen's tent and the Norwegian flag.

To put your clothes on the tent floor, turn to page 146.

To hang your clothes up in the tent, turn to page 148.

You enjoy the swoosh of your skis over the snow. The trip to the Pole is going well. You travel 15 to 17 miles per day.

But this job leaves you tired and hungry. You eat once at midday and again when you set up camp at night. You get a few more extra rations than the dogsled drivers, but it's still not much.

One night during your evening meal, you are in charge of food preparation. You look around to make sure no one is watching. You eat an extra biscuit and a portion of dried meat called pemmican.

But Amundsen sees you. He lectures you sternly. "We must be very careful to eat exactly what has been allowed. If you eat too much now, we won't have enough left for the return journey," he says.

You do have one option to eat more. Amundsen plans to kill 24 of the 42 sled dogs and save the meat for food. But if you kill some dogs, that will leave fewer dogs to pull the sleds and supplies. That could force you all into a dangerous situation.

To advise against shooting the dogs, turn to page 150.

To agree with Amundsen's decision, turn to page 152.

Sled dogs were a big part of Amundsen's plan to reach the Pole.

You enjoy the quiet of sitting behind the dogs as they run through the snow. The trip to the Pole is going well.

In the beginning you traveled just five or six hours each day so as not to tire the men or the dogs. You rested the dogs once each hour. You were able to travel 15 to 17 miles per day. You even crossed the Transantarctic Mountains. The dogs were a big help.

But now Amundsen has a plan for the remaining journey to the Pole and the return journey. He thinks you should kill 24 of the 42 dogs to provide food for the other dogs and for the hungry men who are on skis.

This is difficult news for you. You have grown close to the dogs. You feed them every day, take care of them, and give them commands to go forward. But Amundsen is your leader.

To refuse to help kill the dogs, turn to page **150**.

To help shoot the dogs, turn to page **152**.

To your surprise, Scott sends back only three men. You are one of them.

Five men are going to the Pole. Scott thinks the fifth man will provide more pulling power. But that leaves your team short one man. You will all have to pull heavier sleds with three people than you would with four.

You and your two companions begin your return journey on January 4. You climb over the same terrain and trudge through the same deep snow that you did the first time. You cover only a few miles each day.

The wind blisters your cheeks and fingers. Your feet and hands are so numb you can barely feel them. Your food supply is running low. Your stomach burns with hunger. Many times, you almost faint. But if you stop, you know you'll die. On February 19 you finally stumble into camp.

You rest for several days. You eat as much as you can. You wait for Scott and the four others to return. But as the Antarctic heads toward its winter, you realize that Scott's team isn't coming back. Even if they are still alive out there somewhere, they won't be able to survive the brutal winter.

You must wait several more months for the weather to turn warmer. While you wait, your heart sinks when you hear that Amundsen's team reached the Pole on December 14, 1911. They returned to their base camp in January.

In late October 1912, you set out with a search party to find Scott's team. On November 12 you discover Scott's tent buried in the snow about 11 miles south of the largest supply depot. Inside the tent are the bodies of Scott, Edward Wilson, and Henry Bowers, along with Scott's diary.

Turn the page.

You read the diary and learn that Edgar Evans and Lawrence Oates died before the other three reached their final camp. The diary's last entry is dated March 29. You are grateful that you survived the expedition, but mourn the loss of your leader and friends.

THE END

To follow another path, turn to page 121.
To read the conclusion, turn to page 211.

You look at the sky. Milky, fat clouds straddle the horizon. No doubt the snow will start to fall soon.

A strong blizzard forms as you leave. You struggle against the high winds and heavy snow. But your team is strong. In three days you travel 50 miles. By the end of the third day, the blizzard ends. You easily cover more than 20 miles a day in the good weather.

At the end of the week, you arrive at the base camp. Warm food and your comfortable beds await you. You were not part of the historic journey to the Pole, but you explored other parts of the harsh continent and survived.

THE END

To follow another path, turn to page 121.
To read the conclusion, turn to page 211.

You're tired when you get to the tent. You pile your clothes next to your sleeping bag. In the morning, they are still wet. You have no choice but to put them on.

"We must travel at least 15 miles a day to get back to camp before the weather worsens," Scott says.

Soon you realize that Scott didn't plan for bad weather. He planned only for the exact amount of food he thought your team would need, and you have an extra man. Also, you were not able to lay that last depot of food and fuel.

The men are sick, weak, and exhausted. Your head throbs. Blood trickles from your nose. All of you have nosebleeds from the high elevation.

Soon you fall behind the others. By the time they come back on skis to look for you, you are so confused that you don't even recognize them. The cold and starvation have taken their toll on your body. You feel the other men lift you up and carry you to the tent, but you can't speak.

"Let's give him some warm broth," one of your companions says. He lifts your head, and you try to drink. But you're too tired. All you want to do is sleep. That's the last thing you remember. You are the first of the five men to die on the return journey. Not one of you will make it back to camp.

THE END

To follow another path, turn to page 121.
To read the conclusion, turn to page 211.

You hang up your clothes in the tent. You think getting them off the floor will help them dry quicker. The next morning, the clothes are almost dry.

Scott wants to travel 15 miles a day in order to return to camp before winter begins. You find the depots that had been laid earlier. But there isn't enough food there. You feel weak and move slowly. You fall often. Your legs are bruised and sore from the falls. Temperatures plummet to -40 F.

Because you stayed dry, you fare a little better than the others. Edgar Evans is the first to die. He had severe frostbite and an infected accidental knife wound. Then one day Lawrence Oates leaves the tent. He says, "I'm just going outside, and I may be some time." You all try to stop him, but you are too weak. Now it's just the three of you.

By mid-March it's clear that you will not be able to make it to the next depot. You wished you had made different decisions. But nothing can be done about that now.

You all write letters to your families and leave them in the tent. Scott writes, "Had we lived, I should have had a tale to tell of the hardiness, endurance and courage of my companions which would have stirred the heart of every Englishman." It was a noble effort, but not one of you succeeded.

THE END

To follow another path, turn to page 121.
To read the conclusion, turn to page 211.

"I don't think that's a good idea," you tell Amundsen. "We will need all their power to get us to the Pole and back."

"But the dogs and the skiers are hungry," Amundsen says. "We will travel lighter and save on food if we do this. It must be done."

But you can't stand to shoot the dogs. You let your companions do it. You also refuse to eat the dog meat, even though you know it would give you much-needed energy.

There is little time to rest. You must push on to the Pole. In less than a month, your team arrives. There is no sign that Scott was there. You are the first! Your names will go down in history. You cheer as Amundsen plants the Norwegian flag at the Pole.

You spend a couple of days at the camp before starting the journey back to Framheim. The well-placed depots along the way supply the food and fuel you need. You all arrive back at base camp alive.

But your decision not to eat the dog meat has left you weak. Your body will never be the same again. You live out your life in a weakened condition, but you still are a hero.

THE END

To follow another path, turn to page 121.
To read the conclusion, turn to page 211.

You help shoot the dogs. Some of the men refuse to take part. But you see no choice. You eat the meat and almost immediately feel better.

About three weeks later, on December 14, you finally reach your goal: the South Pole! And even better, there are no signs of Scott's team.

Crew member Helmer Hanssen celebrated with the sled dogs at the Pole.

"We are the first!" you yell. All five of you hug one another. Even the normally calm Amundsen smiles widely.

"Who wants to plant the Norwegian flag?" Amundsen asks.

You look at the others. They are silent. "You should plant it," you say. "You are our leader."

Amundsen places the flag at the Pole. He pitches a small tent. Inside he leaves letters that he wrote for the king of Norway and also for Scott.

After a couple of days of making observations, you head back to Framheim. The team has no problems finding the supply depots. You have enough fuel and supplies to successfully return. After several weeks, you and your team return to Norway as heroes.

THE END

To follow another path, turn to page 121.
To read the conclusion, turn to page 211.

Skiers exploring Antarctica pull their supplies on sleds.

CHAPTER 3

Women making History

You are about to make history. You are leading a group of four women skiing to the South Pole. No other group of women has done this before.

You plan a traverse of the continent. You will start at one end of Antarctica, travel to the South Pole, and then continue to the opposite coast. You'll travel a distance of 1,500 miles. You're all in this together. If for some reason one woman can't finish, the rest of you won't go on.

155

The four of you have raised all the money for the trip. You are on a tight budget. The only way not to go over budget is to stick to a timeline. Your trip is planned to last three and a half months. A delay could make it more expensive to get home. It also puts you at risk of traveling during the dangerous Antarctic winter.

You choose your supplies carefully. You load up about 1,000 pounds of food for the trip, including cheese, beans, pasta, dried meat, and oatmeal. Chocolate, nuts, and dried fruit will be high-energy treats.

Your tents, sleeping bags, and clothes are made of materials such as polypropylene, polyester, and polar fleece. These materials are both lightweight and warm.

Survival equipment includes tents, stoves, and fuel.

You begin your journey on November 9. Immediately, a blizzard flares up. Do you press on and hope the storm ends soon? Or do you stay until it blows over?

To wait, turn to page 158.

To leave, turn to page 159.

Waiting proves to be a good decision. The storm lasts for a couple of days. As you huddle in your tent, you worry about the delay.

"Will we be able to make up this lost time?" asks your tentmate, Jill.

"Yes, I think so," you reply. "But we're going to have to go farther each day than we had planned. It will be tough." You had planned to cover about 5 miles each day in the beginning. You are pulling a 200-pound sled, so it's difficult to travel farther than that.

To push the pace, turn to page **164**.

To make up time later, turn to page **166**.

You wait only long enough for the storm to ease up a bit. By the time you pack up and load the sleds, snow is still whipping through the air. Your muscles ache from the weight of the 200-pound sled. As the trip continues, the sled will become lighter because you'll use up food, fuel, and other supplies. Then you'll be able to travel between 15 and 20 miles each day. But now the weight makes it hard to meet your goal of 5 to 6 miles per day.

After a couple of days, you develop a deep, hacking cough. You think it's bronchitis. The bitter cold, driving snow, and hard work have weakened your body. At night your cough wakes up Jill, your tentmate.

"Maybe we should have waited for the storm to pass," Jill says. "We've pushed too hard. I think we should rest here for a couple of days."

Turn the page.

"I would feel better after resting," you admit. "Then I could start strong and maybe go even farther each day."

But resting would put the whole group behind. What if the group doesn't reach its goal because of you?

To rest for a couple of days, go to page **161**.

To keep moving, turn to page **162**.

The other team members, Beth and Kristine, agree that you should rest.

"We could all use a break," Beth says. "We'll come back stronger."

After a full day and night of sleep, you feel much better. Your cough has almost disappeared. You must decide whether to make up the lost time now, or wait until later in the journey when your sleds will be lighter. Right now, you can travel 5 to 6 miles per day with the heavy sleds. But you could push yourself to go faster. If you increase your mileage now, you will get back on schedule sooner.

To increase the pace, turn to page 164.

To stick with your original plan, turn to page 166.

"I think I'll be OK," you say to Jill the next morning. "Let's keep moving. I'll take some medicine from the first-aid kit."

The first-aid kit contains several kinds of medicine. It also holds bandages and splints. Since you think you might have bronchitis, you take antibiotics.

Two days later, you feel much better. The cough is less noticeable and you have more energy. Your teammates give you a little extra oatmeal and cheese to make you stronger. After a hard day of pulling, the three other women set up the tents and the stove used for food preparation and heat so you can rest.

Two weeks later, you notice the food supplies are getting low. The antibiotics are also almost gone. What if someone else gets sick? There wouldn't be enough medicine for them.

You could use your radio to call for a helicopter to fly over and drop supplies. But that will cost more money—money you don't have.

To arrange for a supply drop, turn to page **170**.

To decide against a supply drop, turn to page **174**.

It is not easy to pick up your pace, but you are strong and well rested. Each day you follow the same routine.

You wake around 6 a.m. and make breakfast on the camp stove. You put on your clothes, pack the gear, and are out of the tent by 8 a.m. It takes another 30 to 40 minutes to pack the sleds. You ski for about two hours, then take a 15-minute break. You ski single file. You do this until about 7 p.m, when you stop to set up camp and cook supper. You're in bed by 10 p.m.

Things are going well until one day, you look ahead and see Beth fall to the ground. You quickly ski to her.

"Ouch!" Beth says, grabbing her ankle. "I hope it's not broken."

As you touch the ankle, Beth winces in pain. Jill and Kristine ski to her side.

"We'll have to make camp here," you say. "There's no way she can keep going."

To rest before continuing, turn to page **168**.

To call off the journey, turn to page **173**.

You decide to continue with your original schedule. As your sleds become lighter, your speed should increase.

But when you are three weeks away from the Pole, you look at the supplies. Something seems wrong. "The food is running very low," you say. "We don't have enough to last us to the Pole."

"How did that happen?" Beth asks. "We've been eating exactly what we rationed."

"I must have miscalculated how much we need," you reply, shaking your head. How did this happen? You planned this expedition in

every detail.

"What are our options?" Kristine asks.

You sigh and think over her question for several minutes. What can you do?

"We can eat less than we're eating now and try to make our food last until we get to the Pole," you reply. "We can pick up supplies there. Or we can try to arrange a food drop in a few days. I have the radio. I can call the base camp to arrange for a helicopter to fly over and drop food down to us. That will be expensive, though."

To arrange for a supply drop, turn to page **170.**

To decide against a supply drop, turn to page **174.**

Scientists have worked at the Amundsen-Scott South Pole Station since 1956.

After a few days of rest, Beth's ankle is less swollen. "We'll divide up your supplies and put them on our sleds," you tell Beth. "That way you'll have a lighter load to pull." That does the trick. You make great progress each day for several weeks.

On January 12 you see some tiny specks on the horizon. Your global positioning system (GPS) shows that you are getting close. What you see is the Amundsen-Scott research station at the South Pole. One more day of skiing, and you arrive! The scientists and workers at the South Pole station greet you with cheers and chocolate.

But you are only halfway through your journey. You still must travel across the other half of the continent. You all are exhausted, and Beth's ankle is still sore. In slightly more than a month, the last ship will leave the coast. If you don't make it in time, you will have to pay hundreds of thousands of dollars to arrange a plane trip home.

You gather the women together. "Let's sleep on it tonight. We'll make a decision about whether to continue in the morning."

To abandon your trip, turn to page 179.

To continue, turn to page 180.

You each need about 5,000 calories a day to give you the energy to ski all day. You turn on the radio and call the base camp each hour to report the latest weather conditions. Aircraft can't land if it's snowing or windy.

During a good stretch of weather, the helicopter lands safely. The pilots bring food and supplies. When you load the sleds the next day, you notice the extra weight. It makes it hard to travel more than 6 to 8 miles each day. You make slow but steady progress.

You arrive at the South Pole on January 13. The dozens of scientists and researchers stationed there are all outside to welcome you. They greet you with hugs. Some hand you chocolate and other treats.

After the fanfare, you go to a quiet place and gather with your team.

As many as 150 people work at the Amundsen-Scott station during the summer months.

"OK, this is just the halfway point," you say. "Do you think we should keep going, even though we're behind schedule?"

"The last ship out of the harbor leaves in just over a month, right?" asks Kristine.

You nod. "If we don't get there in time, we're going to have to pay about $500,000 to arrange for a plane to pick us up."

Turn the page.

Jill shakes her head. "That's money we don't have."

"The weather is going to get worse too," Beth says.

"That's true," you say. "But remember that this is our one shot to make history. No female team has ever crossed the entire continent. It will be an incredible challenge, but if you're prepared to go for it, we have a chance. Let's sleep on it tonight. We'll make a decision tomorrow morning."

To continue, turn to page 177.

To abandon the trip, turn to page 179.

You stop and rest for several days, but Beth's ankle isn't healing. You suspect the ankle might be broken. Your heart is heavy as you call another team meeting.

"I'm so sorry," Beth says. "I just don't think I can go on."

"You're right," you say. "If it gets worse, there is no one who can treat it. You need a doctor."

You use the radio to call the base camp for help. A helicopter swoops in to pick up you and your teammates. You may not have reached your goal, but you're proud that you tried. You vow to someday return to Antarctica and complete the trip you started.

173

THE END

To follow another path, turn to page 121.
To read the conclusion, turn to page 211.

"A supply drop is going to cost us too much money," you say. "We're only about three weeks from the Pole. This will be a tough journey on less food, but we can do it."

But after a few days, you all start to feel the effects of not eating enough. You have been eating about 5,000 calories a day, but now you're trying to live on half of that. You have little energy. Going even 5 miles a day proves difficult. You all have frequent headaches.

With two weeks left to get to the Pole, you call a team meeting.

"This isn't working as well as we had hoped," you say.

"But we've come this far," says Beth. "It's hard to give up now."

The harsh weather is just one enemy of Antarctic explorers.

"That's true," says Jill, with tears in her eyes. "But I think we all know that to keep going while we're weak could result in serious injury or illness."

"Let's face it," Kristine adds. "Death is a very real threat right now."

Turn the page.

You nod. "You're right. As the leader, I'm responsible for everyone. To stop now is a difficult decision. But in order to stay safe and save our lives, it's the right thing to do."

You call a helicopter for rescue. You are ending your Antarctic journey earlier than you had hoped. But traveling as far as you did is a great accomplishment—something most people in the world will never do.

THE END

To follow another path, turn to page 121.
To read the conclusion, turn to page 211.

You're going for the traverse—the trip across the entire continent. You'll be using UpSkis. These sail-like contraptions attach to your body. While you ski, the sail catches the wind. You hope the UpSkis will help you travel much farther each day.

The Upskis work OK, but you're skiing against the wind, so you don't travel as far as you had planned.

"It's clear we're not going to make the deadline," you tell the others. "We're going to miss the ship going out of the harbor. We'll have to call for the plane when we finish our journey."

You celebrate when you reach the coast. But the $500,000 you spend for the airplane to pick you up casts a cloud on your good mood.

Turn the page.

You arrive home as heroes. You travel the country speaking to organizations and schools. But you also have a huge debt that will take many years to pay off. Still, you're glad that you followed your dream.

THE END

To follow another path, turn to page 121.
To read the conclusion, turn to page 211.

The next morning, you gather your team together. Their faces are somber.

"I'm afraid we will not be able to do the traverse," you say. "The risk of something going wrong is too great. I will call for a helicopter to pick us up."

Beth, Jill, and Kristine nod in agreement, although there are tears in their eyes. If you keep going, everyone's lives would be at risk. Your decision to not continue is difficult, but wise.

THE END

To follow another path, turn to page 121.
To read the conclusion, turn to page 211.

The four of you meet in a quiet place to talk over your options. You ask the other women for their opinion s.

"Let's go for it!" Jill says. "I think we're all feeling pretty strong."

Beth and Kristine nod in agreement. "We at least have to try," Beth says.

"And we have the UpSkis," you add. An UpSki is a sail you attach to your body as you ski. The wind catches the sail, carrying you farther faster.

You all set out. To your relief, the Upskis work perfectly. You feel like you're sailing over a vast white ocean. The closer you get to the coast, the happier everyone feels. The difficulties of the earlier journey are almost forgotten.

UpSkis use the wind to increase a skier's speed.

You reach the coast in time to catch the ship.
It's time for another celebration. You have become
not only the first female group to reach the South
Pole, but also the first female group to travel across
the entire continent. You are brave, courageous role
models for generations of women.

THE END

To follow another path, turn to page 121.
To read the conclusion, turn to page 211.

Researchers use devices with underwater cameras to study marine life.

CHAPTER 4

A Modern-Day Adventure

You are a research assistant who studies cold weather. You're starting an exciting mission. You will live and work at the Amundsen-Scott South Pole Station. Modern technology has made it possible for people to travel and stay in Antarctica. During the Antarctic summer, as many as 150 people live and work at the research station.

But one thing hasn't changed since the days of the early explorers. Antarctica remains a vast wilderness. Travelers still face great danger. Blizzards strike without warning. Giant crevasses lurk underneath thin layers of snow. Making the right decisions is the key to survival.

Turn the page.

Emperor penguins are found only in Antarctica.

You arrive at the South Pole and meet your new boss, Jim Potter.

"Welcome to the base!" he says, clapping you on the back. "I hope you're ready."

"I'm excited to be here," you reply.

"That's great," Potter says. "I could use your help in a couple of different ways. You could stay here at the station and help investigators in their drilling and collection of ice cores. The ice samples can contain information on the history of Earth's climate. This information helps scientists learn about today's global warming."

He pauses. "Also, some of our scientists need an assistant for emperor penguin research on one of the continent's islands. You will have to travel away from the base for a few weeks. But some people like getting away from the base, although a trip can pose a little more danger than staying here."

To study the penguins, turn to page 186.

To stay at the base, turn to page 188.

It would be fun to see more of Antarctica. Plus, the nearly 4-foot-tall emperor penguins are one of the few animals that can be studied in a habitat untouched by humans. Scientists study what effect climate change has upon the penguins. In turn, that can help them understand how climate change might affect people.

You board a small airplane with zoologist Wayne Campbell and six other researchers. The plane takes you 900 miles from Amundsen-Scott station to the McMurdo Station, an American research base on the coast of the Ross Sea.

From there, two trips are planned to the nearby island. You can take another plane ride, which will get you there more quickly. Or you can go to the island by boat, which is slower but possibly safer. The weather and extreme cold of Antarctica can affect a plane's performance while taking off, flying, and landing.

Small airplanes help researchers travel through the Antarctic.

To travel by plane, turn to page **189**.

To travel by boat, turn to page **191**.

There's enough exciting work at the South Pole station to keep you busy. After a month, you eagerly await the plane that will bring food and other needed supplies. You look forward to a few treats, such as fresh fruit from New Zealand. But the day the plane is due to land, Jim Potter rushes into the lab. His face is pale.

"What's wrong, Jim?" you ask.

"The supply plane had to make a crash landing!" he exclaims. "One of the pilots left a radio message. They are not too far away. We need to send some people to rescue them. We also need a team here to coordinate the rescue effort and listen to the radio messages. What do you want to do?"

To join the search, turn to page 192.

To stay behind and coordinate the rescue effort, turn to page 193.

You board the LC-130 aircraft, which is equipped with skis for landing on ice. There are no seats. You sit on a bench along the plane's wall. The ride is bumpy and rough. After about an hour, an unexpected snowstorm begins. Strong winds rock the plane back and forth.

"Brace yourself for a water landing!" the pilot shouts over the intercom. You put on the life jacket that is under your seat and put your head between your knees.

Boom! The plane lands roughly in the water but holds together. It bobs in the water a few yards from shore. You're all able to leave the plane quickly. But the shock of the icy water sends shivers throughout your body. The temperature is around 10 F.

"Get to shore!" Campbell shouts. You swim furiously toward land. It's only a short distance, but moving your arms and legs in the icy ocean is almost impossible.

Turn the page.

You arrive on the shore, exhausted and breathless. You're at great risk for hypothermia. You know you should remove your wet clothes and huddle with the others for warmth as you wait for rescue. The pilot had just enough time to radio for help before the crash. But some of the other passengers are already weak and almost unresponsive. They need help.

To remove your clothes before helping the others, turn to page **198**.

To help the others first, turn to page **200**.

A few other researchers also decide to take the boat. It takes about a day to reach the island.

"We're glad you're here!" says zoologist Sarah Jones when you arrive. "Come with me to the rookery to observe the baby penguins."

You spend many hours at the rookery. You walk around and grow warm under your many layers, despite the cold temperatures. You take off your outermost coat and your gloves.

By the time you're finished observing the penguins, you can't even feel your fingers. They are waxy and white. You recognize the symptoms as frostbite. What is the best way to treat it?

To warm your hands gradually, turn to page 202.

To rub your hands to generate heat, turn to page 203.

You and four other workers join the search. You grab a rope and other rescue supplies. You pile on many layers of clothing—a light wool base layer to trap heat, a windproof jacket, and over all of that, a thick parka. You wear two pairs of thermal underwear as well as a pair of snow pants. The pilot is able to communicate by radio, so you know exactly where the crashed plane is located. You should get there in about an hour by snowmobile.

But suddenly the wind picks up and snow begins to fall. In just minutes, a blizzard is raging. It's impossible to see through the thick snow whipping around you.

"Quick!" you shout. "Everyone stop!"

To stay put until the storm lifts, turn to page 195.

To continue the mission, turn to page 205.

You monitor the radios and communicate with both the pilots and the rescue team. After about an hour, the rescue team finds the pilots, who are safe and unhurt.

Your time at the station is almost over as the Antarctic summer draws to a close. One day scientist Ann Smith tells you about an exciting opportunity. "As you know, a few of us stay here during the winter," she says. "It's a small group, but we do some important work. Are you interested?"

You are happy to have this opportunity, so you say yes. In the winter, the sun never comes over the horizon. But this allows you to see the beautiful aurora australis, the Southern Lights. The pink, green, and yellow lights dance in the sky like fire.

Turn the page.

Even in winter, the South Pole station is active with scientists, mechanics, and maintenance workers. At night you relax by watching movies, reading books, and listening to scientists give lectures on their findings.

But temperatures sink to -80 F and sometimes even lower. On a routine trip outside to check some equipment, you forget your gloves. In just a few minutes, your fingers are cold and white. You're in the beginning stages of frostbite.

To gradually warm your fingers, turn to page 202.

To put on gloves and rub your fingers together, turn to page 203.

You know from your winter survival training that you shouldn't try to keep going in a blizzard. "Let's dig a snow trench!" you shout to Joe, the man next to you. He passes the word to the other rescuers.

You all stop. Those of you who brought shovels dig into the snow as deep as you can. Others use snowshoes to dig. You carve out a narrow trench about 5 feet deep.

Snow trenches can help stranded people stay alive in the Antarctic.

Turn the page.

You lie down in the trench for protection. The wind blows over the trench, but you stay warm. It's a good thing you put on many layers of clothing.

The blizzard stops in a few hours. You're able to continue with the rescue. When you reach the crash site, the pilot and co-pilot are huddled in the wreckage. Amazingly, their injuries aren't serious, but they need to get out of the cold. The pilot rides on your snowmobile, while Joe takes the co-pilot. Soon you're back at the base.

In a few weeks, you get the opportunity to leave the base and go on a field mission. One field mission will collect meteorites. The other mission will go to the Transantarctic Mountains. This range separates the western and eastern parts of the continent.

To go to the mountains, go to page 197.

To study meteorites, turn to page 207.

You, four scientists, and several other assistants travel 350 miles to the base of the Transantarctic Mountains by snowmobile. There you set up your camp.

One day you travel with two scientists, Carlos Castillo and Anita Singh, to a nearby mountain. You ski there, pulling a small sled behind you. The snow is smooth. You're making good progress as you pull ahead of the two scientists.

"Slow down!" Singh calls to you. "This land is treacherous. You need to be more careful!"

You're a good skier, and you're enjoying the day. Why should you slow down?

To listen to Singh, turn to page 208.

To keep your fast pace, turn to page 209.

"Let me get out of my wet clothes first, and then I will help," you tell the others.

You take off everything but your thermal underwear. This will allow your skin to dry. You help team members who are having a hard time undoing zippers and buttons.

Once everyone is out of his or her wet clothes, you look around for shelter. You spot a rocky area near the shore. "Over here!" you shout. There you huddle together and wait for rescue.

About two hours later, the weather clears and the rescue plane arrives. Your body temperature is starting to drop. But removing your wet clothes and huddling together has kept all of you warm enough to prevent hypothermia.

The rescue plane brings you all back to McMurdo Station. Two days later you take another plane back to the Amundsen-Scott South Pole Station. You decide to stay at the station for the rest of your trip. One rescue is enough for you.

THE END

To follow another path, turn to page 121.
To read the conclusion, turn to page 211.

You decide to help the others. In a few minutes, you will have some time to attend to yourself.

But removing wet clothes from people who are almost unconscious takes longer than you expected. After just several minutes, your fingers are numb and becoming frostbitten. You manage to remove some layers, but not all of them. You huddle with the others for warmth in a rocky area on shore as you wait for rescue.

But you are not staying warm. In fact, you feel like you're getting colder. As the hours pass, you can't stop shivering. When you speak, your words don't come out correctly. And you're so tired. You just want to go to sleep.

"Hey, don't fall asleep!" Campbell says, grabbing your arm. "You need to stay awake!"

But you barely hear him. The rescue plane arrives and takes you to get medical attention.

But it's too late. You fall into a coma and die of hypothermia. The wet, cold clothes prevented your survival in the Antarctic.

THE END

To follow another path, turn to page 121.
To read the conclusion, turn to page 211.

You know it's best not to rub your fingers together. The action might damage the tissue even more. Instead you put your hands in your armpits. You hope your body heat will warm your fingers.

You go inside the shelter and stand in front of a stove. You warm some shirts by the stove and then wrap them around your hands. It takes a couple of hours, but sensation slowly returns to your fingers. Your fingers burn, but you know that they're going to be OK. You treated the frostbite correctly and just in time. Your remaining time in Antarctica goes off without a hitch.

THE END

To follow another path, turn to page 121.
To read the conclusion, turn to page 211.

You put your gloves on. It seems to make sense to keep your fingers covered. You go into the shelter, stand next to the stove, and rub your hands together vigorously. After about a half an hour, your fingers don't feel any warmer. In fact, they feel and look even worse. One of the scientists, Sarah Jones, sees what you're doing and takes a look at your fingers.

"This is frostbite," Jones says. "We need to get these tight gloves off and wrap your hands in warm, loose clothing. The last thing you want to do is rub your fingers together. That can damage the tissue."

Jones warms the clothes by the stove and applies them to your hands. She does this for several hours, but you still can't feel your fingers. "A doctor will have to take a look at this," she says.

Turn the page.

The weather is good enough to allow a rescue plane to land within a few hours. The plane takes you back to McMurdo Station, where you see a doctor. But the frostbite is too advanced. The doctor must perform an emergency amputation of three of your fingers. For the rest of your life, you suffer the effects of your poor decision.

THE END

To follow another path, turn to page 121.
To read the conclusion, turn to page 211.

You continue with the rescue mission. You all creep forward slowly on your snowmobiles. But in the whiteout conditions, you lose your sense of direction. You start to panic as you realize that you can't see any of the other rescuers.

"Help!" you shout. "I'm lost! Where are you?" But the strong wind swallows your voice. Your group can't see or hear you. They don't know you have become separated from them.

You decide to stop and dig a snow trench, hoping it will protect you from the wind. You scoop out snow as deep as you can with your small shovel and lie down in the trench. But even with the walls of snow surrounding you, you become colder and colder. You start shivering and can't stop. You try to stay alert, but your brain seems frozen and sluggish as well.

Turn the page.

Suddenly, though, you start to feel warm. You begin pulling off layers of clothing and tossing them aside. You don't realize that the effects of hypothermia have reached your brain, making you think that you're not cold. Finally, you sink down into the snow again. As you close your eyes, you don't realize that you'll never open them again.

THE END

To follow another path, turn to page 121.
To read the conclusion, turn to page 211.

You take the field trip to study meteorites that are embedded in the snow and ice. Your camp stove provides heat. The tents are surprisingly warm and comfortable.

You spend a week gathering meteorites. The scientists are pleased with what you have found.

"This will help us discover more about our solar system," says scientist Carlos Castillo. "These might be the best samples we have ever found."

You return to the South Pole station and spend the rest of the season helping the scientists. Sooner than you would like, your Antarctic trip is drawing to a close. You enjoyed your time in the wilderness. You plan to return as soon as you can.

THE END

To follow another path, turn to page 121.
To read the conclusion, turn to page 211.

Singh is right. This area is full of dangerous crevasses, many hidden by snow. You slow your pace. Soon you notice an indentation in the snow. It's a crevasse!

"There's a crevasse here!" you shout. Carefully, you all go around the crevasse. You breathe a sigh of relief. You're glad that you slowed down and took the time to be aware of your surroundings. It likely saved your life.

THE END

To follow another path, turn to page 121.
To read the conclusion, turn to page 211.

You keep skiing at the same pace. Suddenly, your legs fly out from under you, and your body plunges down. You've hit a crevasse! You should have known that this landscape might be full of hidden crevasses.

The rope attached to your sled catches on the edge of the crevasse, preventing you from falling all the way down. The scientists hurry to you.

"Hang on!" says Castillo. "I'm going to get another rope."

Just then, your rope loosens. "I'm going to fall!" you scream. Singh tries to grab the rope, but it's too late. You fall 30 feet into the dark crevasse. Your carelessness has cost you your life.

THE END

To follow another path, turn to page 121.
To read the conclusion, turn to page 211.

On both land and sea, survival depends on good decisions.

CHAPTER 5

A Guide to Survival

Do you have what it takes to survive in Antarctica's harsh and unforgiving climate? Survival on the frozen continent depends upon many things. For one, you have to be physically fit. Your body can withstand the harsh Antarctic climate only if it's in top physical condition.

Mental toughness is just as important as physical strength. You must always think clearly. The best way to think clearly is to remain calm. Although some situations can be scary, it does no good to panic. In Antarctica, panicked thoughts can lead to deadly actions.

Turn the page.

Careful planning will also help to make an Antarctic adventure successful. People who travel to Antarctica plan for months or even years before they leave. Many decisions can help increase your odds of survival. For example, you have to arrive during Antarctica's spring or summer, when the weather is at its best. You must bring the right clothing. You must become familiar with cold weather and the dangers it can bring.

Do you know enough about hypothermia? What are its symptoms? How do you treat it? Do you have the right footwear that will help prevent falls? If you plan on traveling outside, do you know how to recognize dangerous crevasses? Do you know the best way to help someone who has fallen into a crevasse?

Ladders and ropes are used to rescue people who fall into crevasses.

In Antarctica, small problems can quickly become life-threatening. An infection or a broken bone that is easy to treat at home requires special care in Antarctica. You should be prepared for any situation.

Many adventurers have traveled to Antarctica. Survival in this wild place poses an exciting challenge. Sadly, many people have gone to Antarctica and have not returned. But many others have traveled there and have returned to tell their stories of adventure. Those stories inspire others to do the same thing. Perhaps they will inspire you. With enough knowledge and preparation, you may have what it takes to survive Antarctica.

The Antarctic is a dangerous but beautiful place.

REAL SURVIVORS

Apsley Cherry-Garrard

Cherry-Garrard survived Robert Scott's ill-fated expedition to Antarctica in 1911–1912. During the winter of 1911, Cherry-Garrard was one of three men to take a 70-mile winter journey to Cape Crozier to collect emperor penguin eggs. Temperatures sunk as low as -60 F. The men also faced dangerous crevasses and raging blizzards. They were near death when they returned from their journey. Cherry-Garrard wrote a book of his experiences titled *The Worst Journey in the World*.

Douglas Mawson

Mawson, a British explorer, survived a deep plunge into a crevasse in 1913. He had started his journey with two companions. Both died, and Mawson had to travel 100 miles by himself. He killed his sled dogs for food and made the journey on foot. He fell 14 feet into a crevasse before his rope caught on the edge. By sheer courage, strength, and will, he slowly pulled himself up.

Ernest Shackleton

The story of British explorer Shackleton is perhaps the greatest Antarctic survival story. In 1914 Shackleton was on a quest to be the first to cross the Antarctic continent. His ship, *Endurance,* was surrounded by ice shortly after leaving the island of South Georgia. Shackleton and his crew were stranded there for 480 days. Miraculously, not one of the 28-man crew died.

Keizo Funatsu

Funatsu was a member of the International Trans-Antarctic Expedition of 1989–1990. With just 16 miles left of the 3,725-mile journey, Funatsu became separated from the others during a blizzard. He survived by digging a trench in the snow and doing exercises every 20 to 30 minutes to stay warm. After a long night, his teammates found him.

Jerri Nielsen FitzGerald

FitzGerald was the only doctor at the Amundsen-Scott South Pole Station in 1999. In May she discovered a lump in her breast. She performed a biopsy on the lump herself and found that it was cancerous. Through e-mail exchanges with other doctors and medical supplies that were flown in, she was able to start chemotherapy treatment. But it was clear she needed to get expert medical attention to save her life. In a daring rescue, a plane landed on October 16 and carried her away from the station. It was the earliest plane rescue in South Pole history. FitzGerald wrote a book about her experiences titled *Ice Bound*. She died of cancer in 2009.

Survival Quiz

1. If you have frostbite on a body part, how should you treat it?

A. Vigorously rub the body part to restore the circulation.

B. Do nothing. It will recover on its own.

C. Warm the body part slowly and gradually.

2. What should you do if your clothes get wet and you can't get indoors quickly?

A. Remove your clothes and huddle with other people for warmth.

B. Keep your clothes on and drink hot tea.

C. Remove only your outer layer of clothing.

3. What is the best diet for a person traveling in Antarctica by ski or sled?

A. Lots of carbohydrates, such as fruit, bread, and sweets.

B. A mixture of high-protein and high-carbohydrate foods, such as dried meat, oatmeal, cheese, beans, and dried fruit, to provide energy and calories.

C. An all-meat diet.

Answers: C, A, B

Can You Survive

THE

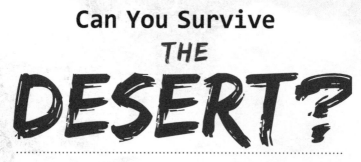

An Interactive Survival Adventure

by Matt Doeden

Consultant:
Marjorie "Slim" Woodruff, PhD
Instructor, Grand Canyon Field Institute

TABLE of CONTENTS

About Your
ADVENTURE

You are lost in the desert, one of the most dangerous places on Earth. Water is almost impossible to find. The daytime sun bakes you with intense heat. The nights can be brutally cold. Venomous snakes and scorpions lurk under rocks.

In this book you'll deal with extreme survival situations. You'll explore how the knowledge you have and the choices you make can mean the difference between life and death. Chapter One sets the scene. Then you choose which path to read. Follow the directions at the bottom of each page. The choices you make will change your outcome. After you finish one path, go back and read the others for new perspectives and more adventures.

YOU CHOOSE the path you
take through your adventure.

Desert plants need little water to survive.

CHAPTER 1

Welcome to the Desert

You're in the desert, one of the least welcoming places on Earth. Water and food are scarce. Temperatures swing wildly from extreme heat to bitter cold. Venomous snakes, scorpions, and spiders lurk in the sand's cracks and crevices.

Deserts cover about 20 percent of Earth's land area. But they're not all hot. Scientists define a desert as any area that receives an average of less than 10 inches of precipitation per year. Because of this fact, the cold continent of Antarctica is considered a desert.

Turn the page.

With so little moisture, deserts can't support
much plant and animal life. Only life adapted to
such harsh conditions can live there.

Deserts are the result of weather patterns. One of the most common is a rain shadow. Rain shadows often form near a large mountain range. Air flows over the mountains. It cools as it rises. As the air cools, its moisture falls on the mountains as rain or snow. On the far side of the mountains, the dry air brings little rain. The area in this rain shadow becomes a desert.

Every continent has deserts. In North America the Mojave and Sonoran cover parts of Mexico and the southwestern United States. Northern Africa is home to the vast Sahara. The Kalahari lies in southern Africa. The huge Gobi desert stretches across Asia, while central Australia holds the Australian Desert. And these are just a few.

Turn the page.

The desert can be a brutal place even for a prepared traveler.

You'll have to figure out how to survive in such a harsh environment. How will you find water and food? Can you avoid deadly wildlife? How can you find your way to civilization and safety? It won't be easy. Are you ready for the challenge?

To take your chances in Africa's Sahara, turn to page 231.

To test your survival skills in North America's Sonoran Desert, turn to page 257.

To see if you have what it takes to survive Asia's Gobi, turn to page 289.

Help can take a long time to reach a desert plane wreck.

CHAPTER 2
Surviving the Sahara

You're half asleep as you gaze out the window of the airplane. Below you lies mile after mile of sand dunes and rocky desert floor.

You're one of just four passengers on the small airplane. It's taking you north toward Cairo, Egypt. There you'll board a jet taking you back home. You've spent two months teaching English to students in small African villages, but now your trip is over. You're eager to return to the comforts of home.

Just as you drift off to sleep, a violent shaking awakens you. The lights in the plane's cabin flicker and die. The plane is dropping rapidly. Something is wrong! Behind you, an elderly woman screams.

Turn the page.

The dull roar of the engines falls silent. With a chill you realize that the plane is going down. You try to take deep breaths. Others in the cabin are panicking. Some are trying to get out of their seats. You check that your seat belt is secure, and then grab the backpack stuffed under the seat.

You remember nothing of the impact. You lose consciousness as soon as the plane hits the ground.

Sometime later you open your eyes. You're groggy, and your forehead is bleeding. A warm, dry wind blows against your face. You're alive! But the good news ends there. The plane ripped into two pieces. You unbuckle and check for other survivors. Everyone else is dead, including the pilot. You are alone and lost in the Sahara Desert.

The plane was small and privately owned. You're not sure if the pilot filed a flight plan. It's unlikely that anyone even knows you're out here.

To stay with the wreckage, turn to page 234.

To gather supplies and search for safety, turn to page 236.

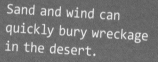

Sand and wind can quickly bury wreckage in the desert.

There's no way you're going to wander off into the Sahara in the middle of the day. The plane's wreckage will provide shelter. Eventually someone will realize the plane is missing and come searching. This is the best place to be found.

In what's left of the cockpit, you find two bottles of water, two bags of potato chips, and a book of matches. You also grab a seat cushion. You gather everything and head outside. You'll use the plane's shadow as shelter. Staying inside with the dead bodies just isn't an option.

The sun dips as evening comes. The air rapidly starts to cool. You build a small fire, using some of the dry brush that grows here as well as the stuffing from the seat cushion.

At dawn you have a decision to make. You're down to a little more than one bottle of water. If you're going to move, it has to be now.

To stay where you are, turn to page 238.

To head in the direction of the lights, turn to page 239.

In what's left of the cockpit, you find two bottles of water and two bags of potato chips. You stuff them into your backpack and head out toward a stand of rocky hills in the distance.

It's late afternoon, and the sun is brutally hot. You dig your baseball cap and a T-shirt out of your pack. You wrap the shirt around your face. Breathing through the cloth will help your body save moisture.

After just 30 minutes, you're already drenched in sweat. Moving over the desert's sand and rock is hard work. You drink from one of the water bottles. You know you will become dehydrated quickly.

Finally you reach the steep, rocky hills. They look difficult to climb. You could keep walking along them, looking for an easier route. But you're eager to climb as high as you can. You hope to see some sign of people.

To search for a safer climbing spot, turn to page 239.

To climb here, turn to page 242.

You can survive here for a few days. You're sure someone will find you by then. You spend the morning going through the wreckage, looking for more supplies. You don't find much. Soon your water is gone. Even in the shade, it's incredibly hot. You're sweating and losing precious moisture every time you move.

Late in the afternoon, you have to empty your bladder. You know that urine is mostly water. You can capture it in your empty water bottle and drink it. But urine is also very salty. Just the thought of drinking it makes you sick. You're not sure you're that desperate. Not yet, anyway.

To capture and drink your own urine, turn to page **246**.

To not risk drinking the urine, turn to page **248**.

You need to get to high ground, but you're not willing to risk a fall that could kill you. You keep walking along the ridge. Half an hour later, you find a much better spot for climbing, with a gentler slope and sturdier rock.

Carefully you scale the rock. You move slowly, taking your time. You examine every handhold and foothold. Snakes and scorpions often make their homes under rocks.

By the time you reach the top, the sun is starting to set. You gather some desert brush and build a small fire. You'll sleep here tonight, just hoping you don't share your bed with an unwelcome critter. After dark you notice glowing lights in the sky to your north. It has to be a city. At sunrise you'll start off in that direction.

Turn the page.

As soon as the sky lightens, you head off toward the lights. You've got one bottle of water left. Walking in the early morning is wise, since the daytime heat will sap your body of energy and moisture. You remember to breathe through your nose. Your body will lose less moisture that way.

Early on you make good progress. The ground here is mostly rocky, covered by dry brush. You see a few signs of animal life—some beetles, a spider, and a few scorpions. You're hungry, but not hungry enough to try eating any of the creatures.

Around noon you spot what looks like a rough road. It's the first sign of civilization you've seen! Excitedly, you pick up your pace and begin to follow the road. But the sun is getting stronger by the minute, and the heat is intense.

You're worried about heatstroke. Your body will begin shutting down if it gets too hot.

On one side of the road is a ridge with a large rock overhang. The shade there would offer a welcome rest, but can you afford to stop?

To continue on the road, turn to page **244**.

To take shelter in the shade until evening, turn to page **250**.

You could walk for miles and not find a better spot to climb. You tighten the straps on your backpack and start climbing.

You make good progress at first. The rock is loose, but you slowly work your way up. Soon you come to a much steeper rock face. It offers plenty of good handholds and footholds. You've always been a good climber, so you don't hesitate. You grab a handhold and start the climb. Before long, you've passed the hard part. Now you're scrambling up the remaining slope on all fours. It's still steep, but much easier.

You reach out to grab a rock that juts up, intending to use it to pull yourself up. "Ouch!" you yelp. A huge scorpion darts out from behind the rock. You pull your hand back, but it's too late. You've just been stung by one of the deadliest scorpions—the fat-tailed scorpion. You'll need to get treatment right away. As you look around, you realize that isn't likely to happen.

You keep moving. But after just a few minutes, the venom starts to move through your veins. Breathing gets more and more difficult. Your vision blurs as you collapse onto the desert floor.

Fat-tailed scorpion stings kill several people each year.

*Turn to page **254**.*

You're on the road to civilization, and you're not about to stop now. You continue on, fighting through the intense heat. Soon your pure water is gone. Your body is showing signs of dehydration. You need to either find water or rescue fast.

Off to one side, you see something shimmering in the distance. It looks like a big body of open water! But heading in that direction will take you away from the road.

To head for the shimmering area, go to page 245.

To continue along the road, turn to page 252.

Your head is aching and your thinking is slowing down. You know that means your body is desperately dehydrated. If there's a chance of finding water, you have to take it.

You stumble off the road. You walk and walk, but never seem to get any closer to the bright, shimmering pool. Dimly, you realize that you're chasing a mirage—a trick of heat and light that only looks like water. You've made a mistake. You have to get back to the road.

You turn around and start to head back, but soon you can't remember which direction is which. As you shuffle along, you trip over a rock and fall hard, turning your ankle badly in the process. You try to stand, but the pain is too great. Finally, you just lie there, panting. You know your body is beginning to shut down.

Turn the page.

Urine contains some body wastes, but it's still mostly water. The problem is that it's very salty—almost like drinking ocean water. If the urine is not concentrated, it's not as bad for you. You've been walking in the hot sun without drinking, though, which makes your urine concentrated. But it might be worth the risk.

You step away from camp and urinate into the bottle. You stand there for a moment, looking at the half-filled bottle. You know that if you look at it too long, you'll lose your nerve. You tip the bottle back and take a drink.

The warm urine tastes about as bad as you expected. You almost choke it back up, but force yourself to swallow.

There's not much more you can do but wait for rescuers. You lie down in a shady spot, but the desert heat is still intense. You're sweating.

Late that afternoon you notice that you're not sweating anymore. At first you think that's good news—it must not be as hot. But the sun is still beating down with incredible strength. Your body has run out of water with which to cool itself.

With no sweat, your body temperature begins to rise. Your skin turns red. You're dizzy and you have a headache. You try to urinate again in a desperate attempt for more liquid, but you can't go. Strangely, you don't really care. In the back of your mind, you know that these are all signs of severe dehydration.

As the sun sets, you close your eyes and drift off to sleep. Some part of you realizes that you won't wake up again.

THE END

To follow another path, turn to page 229.
To read the conclusion, turn to page 319.

Wave your arms or lie down with your hands and legs spread wide so a pilot will see you.

You're not desperate enough to drink your own urine. Urine is saltier than ocean water, and you know that drinking ocean water is deadly. You urinate near a dried bush. Your urine quickly disappears into the rocky, sandy soil.

Day turns into evening. You start to eat the potato chips, but the salt just makes you thirstier. You toss the rest aside, knowing that it's better to be hungry than it is to be thirsty.

By the following day, you are extremely dehydrated. You know you're in trouble when, despite the heat, you stop sweating. That means your body doesn't have any water to spare. You'll be lucky to survive another day.

But that evening you see lights in the sky. With them comes a low humming sound. It's a helicopter! Rescuers have found you! You wave your arms, screaming at the top of your lungs. By staying put and doing what you had to do to stay alive, you've survived your ordeal in the deadly Sahara.

THE END

To follow another path, turn to page 229.
To read the conclusion, turn to page 319.

Continuing to walk in this heat could be deadly. You carefully inspect the area. Finding no dangerous wildlife, you plop onto the ground, enjoying the precious shade. You finish the last of your pure water.

After several hours, the temperature begins to dip. The sun is lower in the sky and not nearly as strong. It's time to move.

You walk for an hour or two when you hear noises ahead. As you come over a small hill, you see people! It's a group of nomads, complete with tents and camels.

You hurry into the small camp. "Help!" you shout, falling to your knees. The surprised nomads yell something back at you, but you can't understand each other.

You grasp your throat and say, "Water, please!" A small boy rushes up with a container of water. As you gulp it, you use gestures to explain the plane crash. You mime using a phone, and they nod in understanding. It seems that they're promising to take you to a phone.

You've made it! Keeping your wits about you has allowed you to escape the deadly Sahara with your life.

THE END

To follow another path, turn to page 229.
To read the conclusion, turn to page 319.

Some desert nomads travel by camel.

Something doesn't seem quite right. What would a huge body of water be doing in the middle of the Sahara Desert? You squint at it and realize that it must be a mirage—a trick of heat and light that only looks like water. There's no help here. All you can do is continue. After about an hour, you collapse onto the ground. Without water, your body is shutting down. Your head aches and your thoughts are slow and confused. Your skin is flushed. You just can't go any longer.

As evening comes, you're drifting in and out of consciousness. You're only dimly aware when a small caravan of nomads spots you. You don't understand them as they try to talk to you, but that doesn't matter. You're still in a daze as they give you water, food, and shelter. The next day they take you to a village, where you can call for help.

A rescue helicopter comes for you and takes you to a hospital in Cairo. Your body has taken a beating. The dehydration has damaged your liver. But you're alive, and you'll heal. You're thankful—you know that even with good decisions, you needed plenty of luck to get out alive. You just wish the others on the plane with you had shared that luck.

THE END

To follow another path, turn to page 229.
To read the conclusion, turn to page 319.

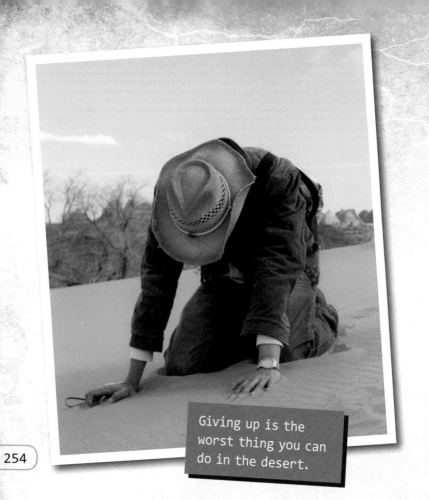

Giving up is the worst thing you can do in the desert.

The pain is unbearable. It's hard to even think straight. You lie there, struggling, knowing that you're in deep trouble. Your mind slips in and out of consciousness.

You wake after dark, shivering. Your breath is coming in short, shallow gasps. Your mouth feels as if it's full of cotton. Your body is fighting with everything it has, but it's not enough. You need water and medical care immediately, and you're not going to get either.

You stare up at the night sky to see the stars, and then close your eyes for the last time.

THE END

To follow another path, turn to page 229.
To read the conclusion, turn to page 319.

The Sonoran Desert covers parts of Mexico, Arizona, and California.

CHAPTER 3

Lost in the Sonoran

It's late afternoon in the Sonoran Desert of northwestern Mexico. What started out as a fun hiking trip with your friends Alex, Jen, and Ruby has turned into a nightmare. While your friends stopped to rest, you decided to take a short hike by yourself. Now you're lost.

You haven't seen the trail for hours. You're alone, with only a small backpack containing a water canteen, a lighter, a pocketknife, your cell phone, and your journal. You left all of your food and other supplies with your friends. Your cell phone isn't getting a signal, and it doesn't seem as if help is coming any time soon.

257

Turn the page.

Rainstorms in the Sonoran are unpredictable.

The only good news you see is dark clouds in the distance. The clouds look as if they could bring rain. That would be a real stroke of luck. Rain would give you a chance to fill your canteen with pure, fresh water. But the storm could easily fizzle out before it gets here. Or it could veer in another direction.

There are only a couple of hours before the sun sets, and you're losing hope that you'll find your friends. Although the late afternoon temperature has to be over 90 degrees Fahrenheit, you know that the desert will cool down quickly, especially if a storm rolls through. You have plenty of time to find a place to camp for the night. But the idea of sleeping alone in the desert isn't very inviting.

Turn the page.

You're at a low altitude, but the landscape is dotted with rocky hills and mountains. If you could get to higher ground, maybe you'd be able to get a cell phone signal. If not, the view from up high might give you a clue of which direction to go for help.

To search for a place to camp for the night, go to page **261.**

To head for higher ground, turn to page **262.**

You don't want to spend a night without shelter, especially in the rain. If you conserve your water, you'll be fine until tomorrow. You have no food, but that's a minor concern. The body can go a long time without food. Water and shelter are your top priorities right now.

To one side a series of narrow canyons dips down below a plateau. The canyon walls would provide some shelter. But should you camp where you're not likely to be spotted? To your other side, the landscape rises gently toward a high ridge. You won't find much shelter there, but even a small campfire might be visible for miles.

To head for the canyons, turn to page **264.**

To camp on the higher, flatter ground, turn to page **267.**

There's often no cell phone reception in the desert.

You head off in the direction of a long ridge. The climbing isn't difficult. The slope is fairly gentle in most places. You're a good enough climber to handle the tougher spots. Within about an hour, you're standing on top of the ridge.

Your luck ends there, though. Your cell phone still isn't getting a signal. You try to figure out a direction to travel but can't see much. You shout at the top of your lungs, hoping your friends can hear you.

With a sigh, you begin the climb back down. You have just enough time and daylight to get back to flat ground. You can't see well enough to build a camp and collect fuel for a fire. A night spent shivering doesn't sound like much fun. You could keep walking. Staying on the move would keep you warm. But in the dark, you run the risk of falling or stepping on a rattlesnake.

To continue hiking, turn to page 269.

To try to sleep here, turn to page 274.

You head toward the series of canyons, grabbing dried brush along the way for a fire. The walls of the canyon will provide a perfect natural shelter.

You find a place to climb down into the deep, narrow canyon. You'll never be spotted here, but the odds of anyone searching for you tonight are low. Even if your friends call for help, the search probably won't start until tomorrow.

The canyon floor was carved by rushing water. Loose rock litters the floor. But finally you find a suitable camp. By sunset you have a small fire going. In the distance you hear the rumble of thunder. A light rain begins to fall. A look at the sky tells you that the heaviest rain is falling to the north, on higher ground. But after awhile a small trickle of water is running down the canyon wall. You easily fill your canteen, drink deeply, and then fill it again.

Steep canyons can flood
in a short time.

Turn the page.

As you watch the water trickling in, you realize that a canyon may not be the safest place to be. Heavy rain could run off quickly and cause a flash flood. But the rain here is light—not even enough to put out your little fire. To abandon your camp now would mean climbing the canyon wall in near darkness.

To abandon your camp, turn to page 272.

To remain here, turn to page 278.

Taking shelter in the canyon is tempting, but it's too dangerous. With storm clouds on the horizon, there's a good chance of rain. In the desert even a little rain can quickly run downhill and create a flash flood.

You settle down on a flat, rocky spot. You won't have shelter, so starting a campfire is especially important. It will keep you warm, and it's possible that someone will spot its light.

You begin gathering desert brush. It feels dry and a bit brittle. You know it will burn easily. You also manage to find the dead husk of a small cactus. This will burn more slowly than the brush and should help keep a small fire going all night. As you're carefully dragging the cactus back to your camp, you hear a sound that no desert hiker wants to hear. It's the rattle of a venomous rattlesnake!

Turn the page.

The rattler is nestled in rocks only a few feet from you. Its body is coiled, with its head and rattles raised in the air. You know the rattle is a warning. If you move away slowly, you should be OK. But you also know that rattlesnakes are almost all meat. You haven't had much to eat today, and your stomach is growling. If you could kill the snake, you'd have the energy you'll need to hike to safety tomorrow.

To slowly back away and return to camp, turn to page **270**.

To try to kill the snake for its meat, turn to page **275**.

With no camp and no fire, you'll be freezing by morning. You decide to keep moving. Walking at night has its advantages. You won't sweat as much, which will conserve your body's water. As you walk, you finish what little water remains in your canteen. You've heard stories of people in the desert dying of dehydration despite still having some water. Conserving water is pointless when your body needs it now.

By dawn you're exhausted. You're more lost than ever, and now you're out of water. Nothing looks familiar. The only sign of civilization you've found is a rusted old motorcycle alongside a small canyon. As you look at the rusty machine, you have an idea. The motorcycle still has tires on it, and burning rubber creates a lot of smoke. You could build a signal fire. The only question out here is whether anyone would see it.

To continue walking, turn to page 283.

To try to build a signal fire, turn to page 285.

You may be hungry, but you're no fool. Picking a fight with an angry rattler is a bad idea. Slowly you back away from the snake. When you're at a safe distance, you turn and dart back to camp.

You use your lighter and a few wadded-up sheets of paper from your journal to get the fire going. Soon you've got a warm little blaze. As the sun sets, you watch the storm approach to the north. You get only a few drops here—not enough even to collect. It looks as if you'd been a few miles north, you'd have gotten a good soaking.

It's a restless night. You have to constantly feed the fire to keep it going. But at least you're warm and safe. At dawn you know it's time to move. It's best to do your walking before the midday heat.

Soon you're out of water and still have no idea where to go. The only sign of civilization you see is an old, abandoned motorcycle. The rusty bike looks like it's been sitting here for years.

The motorcycle does have its tires. You know that tires create a lot of smoke as they burn. They might make a good signal fire. But you're not sure you want to take the time to start a fire.

To continue walking, turn to page **283**.

To try to build a signal fire, turn to page **285**.

Canyon walls are often steep and treacherous.

You need to get out of the canyon now. Flash
floods can be sudden and violent, and you don't
want to be trapped here.

You try to backtrack and find the spot where
you climbed down. But in the dark, you don't
recognize anything. You pick a spot that seems
gentle, groping the canyon walls for footholds
and handholds.

Slowly you work your way up the face of the canyon. You know that a fall now will be deadly. But luck is on your side. Soon the canyon wall begins to flatten out. On all fours, you scramble up out of the canyon and onto flat land. Your hands are shaking as you let out a huge sigh of relief.

Of course, now it's dark. You have nowhere to camp and no way to gather materials for a fire. It's going to be a cold, lonely night.

Turn the page.

You pick a spot on the desert floor and flop down. You curl up to conserve your body heat. A light mist falls from the sky, leaving your clothes damp and making the cold that much worse. You're shivering within an hour. Your body is losing heat quickly, starting to enter a state of hypothermia.

By the time dawn comes, you're almost paralyzed by the cold. All you want to do is stay and wait for the sun to warm you. But it will be several hours before the day really begins to heat up. You should get up and move around, but you're not sure you have the energy.

To get up and start moving, turn to page 280.

To remain here, waiting for the sun to warm you, turn to page 282.

You've seen survival TV shows where people catch snakes for food. All you have to do is grab the snake behind its head and then chop off the head.

You grab your pocketknife. You'll have to move fast. As you step forward, the snake uncoils and strikes. Quickly you step back out of its range. You dart to one side and stomp your foot down on the front half of the snake's body. You try to drive the tip of the knife through its skull, but in your hurry, you miss. A sharp pain burns through your hand and wrist. You've been bitten!

A rattlesnake's rattles are made of keratin—the same substance as human fingernails.

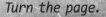

Turn the page.

You step back, stunned. The snake quickly slithers away. You know that rattlesnake bites are rarely fatal, but that's partly because people can get treatment. That's not an option for you. Under normal circumstances, you would probably be OK even without treatment. But your body is already weak from the heat, hunger, and dehydration.

You stumble back to camp and lie down. Your hand is swelling. You're entering a state of shock. You close your eyes, suddenly exhausted. You don't even have enough energy to build a fire.

By midnight, you're shivering. All the heat of the day is lost, and now your body is dealing with hypothermia. You're losing heat more quickly than your body can produce it. Your throat is dry and sore. Your hand feels as if it's on fire. You can't concentrate.

The next morning, the sun rises, but you never see it. It's only a matter of time until rescuers come, but it will be too late for you.

THE END

To follow another path, turn to page 229.
To read the conclusion, turn to page 319.

The heavy rain is miles away. You decide you'll be fine here. You lie down against a canyon wall, near your little fire. Soon you drift off to sleep.

You don't know how long you've slept, but you awaken with a shock. You're wet! A few inches of water is rushing along the canyon floor. Your fire has died, and it's very dark. You leap to your feet. The torrent of water is quickly up to your ankles, and then to your shins. It flows with surprising force.

You begin to panic—there's no way out! The sound of rushing water grows louder. It's up to your knees. The force of the current is already threatening to knock you off your feet. You cling to the canyon wall, but the water just keeps coming. Soon you can't hold on any longer. You shout at the top of your lungs as the current rips you away, but no one can hear you. Too late you realize that in the desert, flash floods can come from rain that falls miles away, especially in low-lying areas.

In the desert, a small creek can quickly become a rushing river.

As the water carries you, your head smashes into a rock. You're groggy and disoriented. Your head goes under. You gasp for breath, and water fills your lungs. You're horrified as you realize that you're about to drown in the middle of a desert.

THE END

To follow another path, turn to page 229.
To read the conclusion, turn to page 319.

With a groan, you pull yourself to your feet. You start walking, hoping that you'll find help.

As the sun climbs higher in the sky, the air grows warmer. You're still cold, but it's getting better. By noon, you're hot. Your water is gone, and your body has stopped sweating. You find a tiny pool of water—only a few sips—and slurp it greedily.

You come upon a narrow dirt road. Your heart races, knowing that you must be getting closer to civilization. About an hour later, you see a cloud of dust approaching. It's a truck. You wave your arms frantically as it approaches. You're filled with joy as it stops.

"Medico, por favor!" you shout. It means, "Doctor, please!" Your Spanish isn't great, but that message is more than clear.

The driver jumps out of the truck and helps you into the passenger seat. Soon you're bouncing down the road with a jug of precious water in hand, headed back to civilization.

It was a close call, but you've made it. You're going to be all right.

THE END

To follow another path, turn to page 229.
To read the conclusion, turn to page 319.

You're so cold that you just want to stay here a little longer. But an hour later, you're even colder. Your skin is pale. You begin to forget where you are and what you're doing. And when your mind clears, it's almost as if you don't care.

A part of your mind knows that these are all symptoms of advanced hypothermia. Your body is losing heat faster than it can replace it.

In time the sun gains strength and begins to warm you. But it is too late. Your body is shutting down, both from hypothermia and dehydration. You know that a rescue party will eventually find you here. But it will be too late. You'll soon be a victim of the harsh Sonoran Desert.

THE END

To follow another path, turn to page 229.
To read the conclusion, turn to page 319.

The large saguaro cactus is native to the Sonoran Desert.

You're miles from civilization. Even a good signal fire might be pointless. You decide that if you're getting out of this desert alive, it'll be on your own two feet.

As the sun climbs higher in the sky, the temperature soars. You breathe through your nose as you move, trying to conserve what little moisture remains in your mouth. At one point you use your pocketknife to cut open a cactus to get at the water inside. But all you succeed in doing is cutting up your hands and getting very little water in return.

Turn the page.

By noon you're starting to feel the effects of severe dehydration. Your body has stopped producing sweat, causing it to overheat. Your mind is getting fuzzy. Making decisions is becoming hard. Soon you just plop down against a rock. Just for a few minutes, you tell yourself. But the desert sun keeps beating down on you. You start fading in and out of consciousness. You realize that you're never going to get up. Your body is so starved for moisture that you can't even shed a tear for yourself.

THE END

To follow another path, turn to page 229.
To read the conclusion, turn to page 319.

You're tired and quickly becoming dehydrated. You won't last much longer. It's time to send a signal. Your friends must have reported you missing by now. People will be looking for you.

You pull the old tires off the motorcycle. You start by building a small fire with pages from your journal and a big pile of dry desert brush. Once it's hot, you carefully arrange the tires on top of it.

Turn the page.

As the tires catch fire, they release huge plumes of thick, black smoke. The smoke rises up into the clear desert sky. You sit down in the patch of shade provided by a large rock. If this doesn't work, you know you're in deep trouble.

But your fire does work. After an hour or so, you hear a deep thump-thump-thump. You look in the sky and see a rescue helicopter. You lie flat on your back and spread your arms and legs wide. That way the pilot is more likely to see you. She does!

As the helicopter lands several yards away, you sigh with relief. You've kept your wits and managed to escape the desert with your life.

THE END

To follow another path, turn to page 229.
To read the conclusion, turn to page 319.

Helicopters are used for rescues because they don't need a runway to land.

Dry lake beds cover parts of Asia's vast Gobi Desert.

CHAPTER 4

Alone in the Gobi

Your heart sinks as your dirt bike sputters and dies. This isn't good. You're alone in the middle of Asia's enormous Gobi Desert. You're spending the summer here with your parents while they study the region's ecology and wildlife. Riding the dirt bike is your favorite pastime. You're supposed to tell your parents if you travel more than a mile or two from your camp, but some days you forget. This is one of those days.

You've been riding the bike along the region's many dry, salt-covered lake beds. A quick guess tells you that you're at least 20 miles from camp. Nobody knows that you're here. They won't miss you until sunset, which is several hours from now.

Turn the page.

The Gobi's sand dunes are popular with dirt bike riders.

You have no water or food. The dirt bike's saddlebag contains only a few items—emergency matches, a pocketknife, a roll of plastic food wrap, and some trash from a long-ago meal. What's worse is you don't know exactly how to get back to camp. Your motorcycle has a GPS that usually gets you home, but the bike's battery is dead. With no power, the GPS is useless.

Your options are limited. You could set out on foot, hoping you're going in the right direction. Or you could camp here, knowing that your parents will launch a rescue effort as soon as they realize you're missing.

To start walking in hopes of finding your way back to camp, turn to page **292**.

To camp here and prepare a fire for the night, turn to page **294**.

You gather your supplies and strike out. Even though the Gobi is a cool desert, the summer sun is warm. You figure that you can cover 20 miles in five or six hours. The only question is whether you're going the right way.

The desert is filled with rocks and dried lake beds. You spot a few small saxaul trees and small bits of dry brush, but little else.

If you find a trail in the Gobi, it's best to follow it.

After an hour of walking, you come across what looks like a trail. Animals have beaten down the ground here. You believe it's a caravan trail. Many of the Gobi's people are nomads. They use camels to move through the desert. If this is a trail, it might lead to help. But the trail heads off in a different direction. You don't think it's the way back to your parents' camp.

To follow the trail, turn to page **295**.

To ignore the trail and continue looking for your parents, turn to page **296**.

By tomorrow your parents will be looking for you. All you have to do is stay alive until they find you. Walking into the desert alone, with few supplies, probably isn't the best way to do that. You'll camp here and wait for rescue.

Nearby are several large boulders. It's the perfect spot. If you camp there and build a small fire, the boulders will trap some of the heat and keep you warm. But gathering fuel for the fire will take a long time—there's not a lot to burn out here. Maybe that time would be better spent searching for water. Without water, you won't last long.

To search for water, turn to page 297.

To work on building a fire, turn to page 298.

This trail is the first sign of civilization you've seen so far, and you're not about to leave it. You choose a direction and start off. Maybe you'll find a small settlement somewhere. Or maybe a group of nomads will come along.

After two hours the trail remains deserted. Did you make a mistake? You're sure now that you're heading in a direction away from your parents' camp. Every step you take will make you that much harder to find. The sun will set in an hour or so. You could continue on the trail through the night. Or you could climb a nearby ridge to see if you can spot your parents' camp from above.

To try climbing for a better view of your surroundings, turn to page 310.

To stick to the trail, turn to page 312.

You're sure the trail leads away from your parents' camp. So you continue the way you were headed. Another hour passes. Nothing looks familiar. You're getting thirstier. And the sun is sinking low in the sky.

A tall ridge is ahead. From the top of the ridge, you might be able to see some sign of civilization. But it looks like a dangerous climb, and there isn't much daylight left. It might be safer just to camp here for the night.

To camp, turn to page **298**.

To climb the ridge, turn to page **310**.

Water is your top priority. Without it, you won't last more than a couple of days. But where can you find water in the middle of a desert?

You scan the landscape. The soil is loose and dry. In the distance you see a thick bunch of vegetation along low-lying land. Plants usually grow where there's a water supply.

Another option is to build a solar still. Your dirt bike's saddlebag holds everything you need to build one—a soda can and a roll of plastic wrap that you use to wrap sandwiches. But you have never built a solar still before. You're not positive it will work.

To work on a solar still, turn to page 300.

To dig for water, turn to page 304.

The Gobi gets very cold at night. You'll need a fire to keep warm. As long as you conserve energy and your body's water, you'll be fine until tomorrow.

You set out to gather fuel. You find a patch of small saxaul trees. You break off several of the small branches. You also peel off some bark from the tree's trunk. There's moisture behind the bark, and you lap it up. It's not much, but you're happy for any drop of water you can find.

Soon you have a nice pile of fuel for your fire. You keep the fire small. You don't want to run out of fuel too soon.

As your fire burns, you decide to get one more load of fuel. You find a bunch of small, dry brush and begin pulling it up. But suddenly, you notice something that makes you freeze in place. It's a snake—a central Asian pit viper! It's one of the deadliest snakes in the world.

Saxaul shrubs and trees are plentiful in the Gobi Desert.

To slowly back away and return to your fire,
turn to page **303**.

To try to chase the snake away with a stick,
turn to page **307**.

Digging for water could be a lot of work with no reward. You'll try your luck with a solar still. You start by digging a hole a few feet deep. It's not hard to do in the dry, loose soil. You find a sharp rock and make cuts in the top of the soda can. You then rip off the top, forming a cup.

Next you need to add moisture to the bottom of the still. Your dirt bike's radiator contains water for cooling the engine. The water could be tainted, so drinking it directly is a bad idea.

Instead you disconnect the radiator and dump the water into the hole you've dug. Then you place your cup at the bottom and cover the hole with the plastic wrap. You weight down the plastic with rocks so it doesn't blow away. You add one small rock to the middle, creating a small dip. Water will drip down to the dip and then into the cup. You finish the job and cross your fingers.

Solar Still

1. transparent plastic

2. stones to hold plastic in place

3. container to catch fresh water

4. non-drinkable liquid

5. sunlight

6. evaporation

7. condensation dripping from the bottom of the plastic

Turn the page.

It's time to gather materials to burn. There's not much available out here. It's going to be a pretty pathetic campfire.

Around sunset you check the still. It's working! A small sip of pure, clean water has collected in the cup. It's really not much water, but it feels like a major victory.

It's a long, cold night. Your fire goes out before dawn. But you're alive.

Turn to page **315.**

You know that if you leave the snake alone, it will most likely leave you alone. You back away very slowly, taking care not to startle the viper. It watches you closely and then quickly slithers away in the opposite direction.

With a deep sigh of relief, you return to your camp. You tend your little fire, which keeps you warm for most of the night. You're hungry, thirsty, and uncomfortable, but all things considered, you're doing quite well. After what seems like forever, you see light on the horizon. The sun is finally rising.

Turn to page **315.**

Nighttime temperatures in the Gobi can drop below freezing, even in summer.

There's a good chance you can find water if you dig in a low-lying area. You head down into the small depression and get to work. At first it's easy. But as you dig deeper, the ground becomes firmer. You have to work harder.

You're breathing heavily from the effort. Your body is dripping with sweat. "Just a little deeper," you tell yourself. But after almost an hour of hard digging, the ground is still bone dry.

You step back, wiping the sweat from your brow. You notice your hands are shaking. You've made a terrible mistake. All that hard work has used much of your body's water reserve. Now your clothing is soaked in sweat, and the sun is setting.

With no time or energy to build a fire, you huddle in a spot where two small boulders form a natural windbreak. But the temperature in the Gobi drops drastically after sunset. You shiver in your sweat-soaked clothing.

Your throat is dry and scratchy. You know you're suffering from early signs of both dehydration and hypothermia.

Turn the page.

It's a long and miserable night. At sunrise you know you should build a signal fire, but you don't have the energy. At one point late in the day, you see a trail of dust in the distance. It's a vehicle! You stand to run toward it, but as soon as you get up, you feel dizzy. Before you realize it, you're face down on the ground. You've fainted. With so little water, your heart is having a hard time pumping blood to your brain.

You've banged your head against a sharp rock. Everything is fuzzy, and your head is bleeding. The vehicle is gone. The driver never saw you.

You fall to the ground. You lie there exhausted, dehydrated, and bleeding. You'll do all you can do to stay alive, but your body's resources are almost spent. The desert has beaten you, and you've probably just missed your only hope of rescue.

THE END

To follow another path, turn to page 229.
To read the conclusion, turn to page 319.

You've found fuel here, and you don't want to give it up. You grab a long, solid piece of brush and wave it at the snake.

But the snake doesn't turn away. Instead, it flattens its body and begins shaking its tail. You shout at the snake and swipe at it with your stick again. But you've forgotten something important. The central Asian pit viper is an aggressive snake. It was warning you to back away. In the blink of an eye, the snake strikes. You've been bitten in the leg! You yelp in pain and run back to your fire.

You soon feel the effects of the venom. Your vision blurs, and you begin to see double. You're sluggish, and every muscle in your body hurts. You lie down and groan in pain. The snake's bite isn't usually fatal, but in this situation, it's big trouble. Your body is without food and water. Your natural defenses are weakened.

Turn the page.

The central Asian pit viper's venom causes pain and muscle paralysis.

You stop tending your fire, and it burns out. That leaves you shivering as the night grows colder and colder.

By morning you can't even get up. Everything hurts. You lie there, waiting for rescue. But you're lying against a boulder, largely hidden from view. You don't have a signal fire to tell rescuers where you are. Meanwhile, your body is losing more and more precious moisture. Soon you're fading in and out of consciousness. Late that afternoon, you lose consciousness for the last time. Your desert adventure is over.

THE END

To follow another path, turn to page 229.
To read the conclusion, turn to page 319.

You're a good climber, so a little ridge doesn't scare you. At first the climbing is easy. But soon the ridge grows steeper. Several times rock breaks away under your hands or feet. You have to scramble to keep from tumbling down the slope.

The climbing makes you sweat. You know your body is using up precious water. But if you can find your destination from up here, it will all be worth it.

As you pull yourself up and scan the horizon, you almost shout with joy. It worked! Far off in the distance, you can see your parents' camp! You carefully make note of the direction, then start down the far side of the ridge.

You soon realize your mistake. This side of the ridge is very difficult to climb. And now the sun is setting, making it hard to see handholds and footholds. In one spot where the slope is almost a sheer drop, the rock crumbles beneath your feet.

Before you realize what's happening, you're falling! It's not a long fall, but as you crash into a rock ledge below, you lose consciousness. When you wake, it's dark. You groan with pain—both of your legs have been shattered in the fall. The bone in your right leg juts out through your jeans. The pain is so intense that you momentarily black out again.

Weakly, you shout for help. But you know that no one will hear you. And on the face of this ridge, there's almost no chance anyone will see you. You close your eyes, knowing your fate has been sealed.

THE END

To follow another path, turn to page 229.
To read the conclusion, turn to page 319.

It's tempting to climb, but staying here may be your best bet. You can walk through the night. That will keep you warm. If you don't find anything by tomorrow, you can build a signal fire.

You're shocked at how dark it is out here. You have only a sliver of moonlight to guide you. But as you squint and look ahead, you notice something. There's a flicker of light up ahead. It looks like firelight.

You move carefully, watching your step in the dark. There's definitely a fire ahead! Soon you hear voices as well. You've found a caravan! You can hardly believe your luck—this is one of the most sparsely populated areas in the world.

You shout out as you approach, not wanting to frighten the people. "Hello! I need help!"

The nomads look at you at first with suspicion. They don't speak English and probably aren't used to running into strangers out here. But soon they see the shape you're in.

Gobi nomads raise camels, along with horses, cattle, sheep, and goats.

Turn the page.

A man rushes out to you and takes you by the arm. He speaks, but you can't understand him any better than he understands you.

Still the nomads seem to understand your situation. They rush to bring you water and food—noodles and what you think is boiled mutton. You've heard that the local people are famous for their hospitality, and you see that it's true.

You still have a long way to go—you may have to find a town or village to call your parents. Your desert journey isn't over yet, but now you know that you'll be OK.

THE END

To follow another path, turn to page 229.
To read the conclusion, turn to page 319.

You've made the best of your situation so far, and today you're hoping all that work pays off. Now that the sun is up, you know your parents will be looking for you. You need to help them find you. You search for materials to burn. After a few hours, you have a sizable stack of vegetation. But most of it is dry. It won't produce much smoke.

Once again you look to your dirt bike for a resource. The bike's motor needs oil to run smoothly. And motor oil makes lots of black smoke when it burns. You drip the oil over the fuel you've gathered. You even soak some sand in gasoline. The fire lights quickly and sends up big plumes of smoke. The smoke rises. If your parents are anywhere nearby, they're bound to see it.

Turn the page.

All you can do now is wait. Soon the fire starts to die down. It's giving off less and less smoke. You throw everything else you have onto it, knowing that this is your best shot. And it works. Within 10 minutes you see a trail of dust rising in the distance. It's your father's jeep!

"Dad!" you shout as you wave your arms. You've never been so happy to see him. You've survived your ordeal in the Gobi Desert. You can't wait to tell your friends about your adventure.

THE END

To follow another path, turn to page 229.
To read the conclusion, turn to page 319.

Desert oases provide food, shade, and water to travelers.

CHAPTER 5

Stay Alive

The desert can be a beautiful and fascinating place. But it's also full of danger. Extreme temperatures, dangerous wildlife, and lack of water can add up to disaster quickly. Time isn't on your side. Your body can go weeks without food, but you'll die in a matter of days without water. If you're sweating and working hard, you'll die even sooner.

Survival in the desert starts with your mind. You have to plan. You've got to collect what resources you have and use them effectively. If you've got water, don't just save it. Your body can go into a state of severe dehydration before you even realize it's happening. Many people in such situations have died with water still in their canteens. Stay hydrated!

Turn the page.

Staying hydrated is the best thing you can do to survive the desert.

It's important that you remain calm. If you panic, you'll make bad decisions. You've also got to maintain the will to live. As soon as you give up hope, you're all but finished. Stay positive and focused on the goals at hand—staying alive and finding rescue.

Always be aware of your situation. Any time you go alone into the desert or other remote location, it's best to tell someone what you're doing and where you are going to be. If you've done that, it may be best to stay put. Find a spot with some shade. Avoid any activity that will make you sweat and lose precious water.

But if nobody knows where you are, you'll have to consider other options. Rescue isn't coming to you, so you'll have to go find it. You might signal for help with a fire, or you might have to take off in search of civilization.

Desert roads are usually not well-marked and may end without warning.

If that happens, look for roads. If you find one, stay close to it. Roads lead to people. And there's always the chance that someone will drive by.

Every decision you make in the desert can be the difference between life and death. Making the right choices isn't easy. Could you eat bugs, snakes, or scorpions? Could you use the materials around you to build shelter and fire? Could you stay positive and focused even when everything seems to go against you?

If you can answer "yes" to these questions, you might have what it takes to get out of a desert alive.

REAL SURVIVORS

Mauro Prosperi

In 1994 Mauro Prosperi was running in a race across the Sahara when a sand storm caused him to lose the trail. Prosperi had little water and no food. At one point he managed to catch two small bats. He killed the animals and drank their blood. He walked toward a mountain range until a small band of nomads spotted him and took him to a nearby village. Prosperi spent six days in the desert and lost 33 pounds. He survived, but extreme dehydration caused severe damage to his liver.

Aron Ralston

In 2003 Aron Ralston went alone into the Utah desert to hike and climb in its long system of canyons. But as he climbed, a large boulder fell, pinning his arm to the canyon wall. He couldn't move his arm or the boulder. He was trapped in the canyon with little food or water for more than five days. Finally, he used a cheap pocketknife to cut off his own arm, freeing him from the boulder. Hungry, dehydrated, and bleeding, he hiked out of the canyon. With one arm, he managed to rappel down a cliff, where he found a small pool of water. He hiked back toward a road until he found a family of hikers, who called for help. Ralston wrote a book about his ordeal, which was later made into the movie *127 Hours*.

Henry Morello

In 2011 Henry Morello was driving home from a restaurant through the Arizona desert when he took a wrong turn. Morello, 84, got stuck in a ditch on a remote road. He was stranded for five days. His car battery and cell phone battery were dead. He took metal parts off of his car and placed them on the roof, hoping they'd reflect the sun's rays and be seen by rescuers. During the cold nights, he used his car's floor mats as blankets. He even drank windshield wiper fluid. Rescuers found him and rushed him to the hospital, where he recovered.

SURVIVAL QUIZ

1. What is your most important resource in the desert?

A. Food

B. Water

C. Shelter

D. Fuel for a fire

2. If you encounter a deadly snake, how should you deal with it?

A. Try to kill it for food

B. Wave your arms and scare it away

C. Back away slowly, making no sudden movements

D. Ignore it

3. Where do many dangerous desert snakes and scorpions make their homes?

A. In desert trees or shrubs

B. Deep in underground caves

C. On top of mountains

D. Under rocks

AUTHOR BIOGRAPHIES

Matt Doeden

Matt Doeden is a freelance author and editor from Minnesota. He's written numerous children's books on sports, music, current events, the military, extreme survival, and much more. His books *Sandy Koufax* (Twenty-First Century Books, 2006) and *Tom Brady: Unlikely Champion* (Twenty-First Century Books, 2011) were Junior Library Guild selections. Matt began his career as a sports writer before turning to publishing. He lives in Minnesota with his wife and two children.

Allison Lassieur

Allison Lassieur has written more than 100 books on many topics, including history, biography, science, and current events. She has also written fictional novels and short stories, puzzles, and activities. When she isn't busy writing, Allison enjoys knitting, spinning, and reading good novels. Allison lives in Trenton, Tennessee with her husband, daughter, and a houseful of pets.

Rachael Hanel

Rachael Hanel was born in Minnesota, where she still resides. She's the author of *We'll Be the Last Ones to Let You Down: Memoir of a Gravedigger's Daughter*, and you're likely to find her roaming around cemeteries.